✓ S0-BYH-523

KNOWLEDGE UNLIMITED PUBLISHING

Presents For Review

MANIC - DEPRESSION : ILLNESS OR AWAKENING

Publication Date : July 4th 1995
Edition : First
Number in Print : 5000

Specifications : 266 pages, 5 1/2 x 8 1/4 trim
with four color and laminated cover

CIP/ LC : QBI94-1321 / 94 - 066741

ISBN : 0 - 9639451 - 4 - 9

Promotional Plans :
$10,000 promotional budget
Space advertising, direct mail and major author tours

TO ORDER CALL : BOOKMASTERS 1-800 - 247 - 6553

A copy of your review to the address below would be appreciated
Knowledge Unlimited Publishing
P.O. Box 707, Bedford Hills, New York, 10507

MANIC-DEPRESSION

ILLNESS OR AWAKENING

Manic-
DEPRESSION

ILLNESS

OR

AWAKENING

ROBERT E. KELLY

KNOWLEDGE UNLIMITED PUBLISHING

BEDFORD HILLS, NEW YORK, U.S.A. 10507-0707

Project Management: J. Carey Publishing Service
Editing: Marjorie Pannell
Text Design: Patrice Sheridan
Cover Illustration: Stephen Marchesi
Text Illustrations: Adventure House

Library of Congress Cataloging-in-Publication Data
Kelly, Robert E., 1954—
    Manic-depression : illness or awakening / Robert E. Kelly.
    p. cm.
    Includes bibliographical references and index.
    ISBN 0-9639451-4-9

    1. Kelly, Robert E., 1954- 2. Manic-depressive psychoses—
Patients—Biography. 3. Spiritual life. I. Title.

    RC516.K45 1995   616.89'5'0092

QBI94-1321

ISBN 0-9639451-4-9
Printed in the United States of America
10   9   8   7   6   5   4   3   2   1

To my parents, Joseph and Joan Kelly
for creating a home grounded in love

To my brother Paul
whose death swept me to heaven
and the pain that brought me back

To my brothers Kevin, Jimmy, and Mark
who gave me their strength
when I had none of my own

To my sisters Debbie and Tara
whose humor made the
tough times bearable

and

To Sarah Kelly
who knows a wizard
when she sees one

Contents

We are not human beings having a spiritual experience,

we are spiritual beings having a human experience.

PIERRE TEILHARD DE CHARDIN

Preface

At age twenty-three, I was diagnosed as having manic-depression. I was hospitalized for ten days, then released. Over the next fifteen years, I had a manic or hypomanic episode about every four years. The results were always the same. I was told to take lithium or risk re-hospitalization, and to undergo therapy to help me deal with my "condition." In this fashion I was labeled, categorized, and dismissed by the medical profession. The doctors wouldn't have to worry about mania again until another psychologically disturbed individual showed up in their emergency room.

There is another point of view regarding what mania is, and a different way of understanding its psychic expression. I am not downplaying the value of the external controls—chiefly drugs—the doctors provided to help rest my mind and body during my manic episodes. I do, however, think this approach is severely limited and does not at all address what mania is. If doctors do not know what mania is, they cannot advise on how to deal with it.

In the second point of view, mania presents to the conscious mind of the individual the immense powers and hidden life of the psyche. I can think of no better way to describe this experience than as an awakening. The psyche, usually obscured by the drudgery and assumptions of our quotidian existence, makes an imperious claim to be known. The individual is awakened to his or her own nature as a spiritual being.

Some people are fortunate to reach psychic awareness after a long course of personal therapy with a psychically inclined therapist. The end result is the same. The difference is that during mania, the revelations of the psyche—difficult to describe except as a sense of universal oneness in all things—come at an accelerated pace, and the individual is usually abandoned by family and friends to endure this experience alone.

With the surcease of mania, these revelations pass, leaving only their memory, and questions. The individual who has had a manic episode has had enlightenment thrust upon him, but not in a form that he can use. His self-doubts increase. He is shunned as "sick." It takes years of work to learn how to access the psyche appropriately. But the experience of awakening, in whatever form it takes, is with the individual forever. It does not matter how you get to that experience. The experience itself is what counts.

Other cultures, even in modern times, seem to have better means of handling awakenings than our society. In India, when an awakening occurs, the individual, if he is living in an ashram, is watched closely. He is taken care of, mentally and physically, by his guru so that he does not harm himself or others. In Mexico the Toltec culture refers to psychic awakening as "the movement of the assemblage point." Under the guidance of a nagual, the individual is instructed and watched so that no harm can occur. In certain Native American cultures, the correlate of psychic awakening is the vision the individual experiences when he goes "up to the hill." In all of these settings, the individual has some preparation for the experience; he may have been instructed, and he has developed discipline through physical and mental training that will see him through the experience. Always, he is guided by a teacher, a man of knowledge.

In contemporary American society, sudden psychic awakening is considered an illness. There is no social support for the individual, who is treated in psychiatric wards with drugs and other remedies intended to "heal" him. Neither the doctor nor the patient knows what is happening or how to handle it. Even when the medical profession's efforts are undertaken with care and concern, the result is usually more harmful than helpful. The problem is compounded by the psychological disturbances that may accompany a sudden insight into one's spiritual being. These disturbances may appear no different, on the surface, from the psychological disarray of true illness, but the causes of the symptoms are vastly different. It takes a gifted therapist, one who has herself traveled the road toward psychic enlightenment, to help you in your search. And you must find that person for yourself.

I've always enjoyed the analogy of the body to a car. When you purchase a new car, you don't have to know how it works. You don't even have to know how to drive it. If the car breaks down, a professional mechanic can fix it for you. To fix the car yourself, you will have to learn what makes the car work. The more you learn, the better you will be able to understand and correct problems as they arise.

The same is true for the body. You can relinquish control to a professional healer, a doctor. Or you can heal yourself, provided you have the knowledge necessary to the task.

It is within this framework that I have come to write this book. My car broke down and, not understanding how it worked, I found someone to fix it. But it wasn't fixed right. It ran, but not as it should. So I went to school to find out what I didn't understand. This work is the result.

A note on the pronouns used in this book: I frequently use "he," rather than "he or she," or even "they," in the first instance to avoid the cumbersome repetitions that result from the lack of an egalitarian pronoun in English to refer to individuals of either sex, and in the second instance because the experience of awakening is intensely individual: It is not a plurality or a mass movement. I am male, and much of my personal work has been concerned with maturing the masculine psyche. The stages of psychic growth are, however, the same for all individuals, everywhere; and I invite women readers to "read" themselves into the situations I describe and supply the nuances of the female experience from their own, personal lives. As psychic growth transcends sexual differences, so we may hope for a better dialogue between women and men once we have better knowledge of ourselves as spiritual individuals.

Acknowledgments

Grateful acknowledgment is made to the following authors and publishers for permission to reproduce material for this book. Any omissions that are brought to this author's attention will be corrected in future editions.

American Psychiatric Association. *Diagnostic and Statistical Manual of Mental Disorders, 3rd. ed.* Washington, D.C.: American Psychiatric Association, 1987.

Assagioli, Roberto. *Act of Will.* New York: Viking Penguin, 1973.

Assagioli, Roberto. *Psychosynthesis.* SterlingLord Literistic, Inc., New York: Viking Penguin, 1965.

Bly, Robert. *Iron John.* Reading, MA: Addison-Wesley Publishing Company, 1990.

Bryson, John (ed.). *Matthew Arnold: Poetry and Prose.* Cambridge, MA: Harvard University Press, 1970.

Campbell, Joseph and Moyers, Bill. *The Power of Myth.* New York: Bantam Doubleday Dell Publishing Group, Inc., 1988

Dumont, Theron Q. *The Power of Concentration*. Homewood, IL: Yoga Publication Society, 1918.

Dumont, Theron Q. *The Master Mind*. Homewood, IL: Yoga Publication Society, 1918.

Fieve, Ronald R. *Moodswing*. New York: William Morrow & Co., Inc., 1975.

Huxley, Aldous. *The Doors of Perception*. New York: HarperCollins Publishers, Inc., 1982.

Jamison, Kay Redfield. *Touched with Fire: Manic-Depressive Illness and the Artistic Temperament*. New York: Free Press, 1993.

Jung, Carl. *The Archetypes and the Collective Unconscious, Number 9: Part 1*. Princeton, NJ: Princeton University Press, 1969.

Jung, Carl and Kerenyi. *Introduction to a Science of Mythology*. Princeton, NJ: Princeton University Press, 1951.

Kast, Verena. *Imagination as Space of Freedom*. New York: Fromm International Publishing Corporation, 1993.

Keirsey, David and Bates, Marilyn. *Please Understand Me*. Del Mar, CA: Prometheus Nemesis Book Company, 1984.

Mandell, Marshall and Scanlon, Lynne. *Dr. Mandell's 5-Day Allergy Relief System*. New York: HarperCollins Publishers, Inc., 1979.

Maslow, Abraham H. *The Farther Reaches of Human Nature*. New York: Viking Penguin, 1971.

Meditations on the Tarot. Rockport, MA: Element Books, 1985.

Moore, Robert and Gillette, Douglas. *King, Warrior, Magician, Lover*. New York: HarperCollins Publishers, Inc., 1990.

Moore, Robert and Gillette, Douglas. *The King Within*. New York: William Morrow & Co., Inc., 1992.

Moore, Thomas. *Care of the Soul*. New York: HarperCollins Publishers, Inc., 1992.

Ouspensky, P.D. *Tertium Organum*. New York: Random House, Inc., 1920.

Peale, Norman Vincent. *Enthusiasm Makes the Difference*. Englewood Cliffs, NJ: Prentice Hall, 1967.

Stallone, James and Migdal, Sy. *Growing Sane*. Dallas, PA: Upshur Press, 1991.

Yates, Frances A. *Giordano Bruno and the Hermetic Tradition*. Chicago: University of Chicago Press, 1964.

A Boundary Broken

FIRST EPISODE

The wind blows where it wills, and you

hear the sound of it, but you do not know

whence it comes or whither it goes; so it

is with every one who is born of the spirit.

JOHN III:8

In the fall of 1977 I was twenty-three years old and a student at the University of New Haven, in Connecticut. Money being scarce, I applied for a job as a security guard. The hours were long and the schedule erratic, but the situation seemed manageable until a series of alternating day and night shifts disrupted my usual sleep patterns. I was unable to sleep after many nights off work. In the aftermath of these disruptions, I began to experience small panic attacks. I would cry uncontrollably for no apparent reason. I tired easily and felt confused.

Most of the sleepless nights I suffered were just long, but one November night was to change my life forever. I had just come off a double shift at work and gone straight to bed. I was so tired I couldn't sleep. As I lay in bed trying to rest, my mind raced with thoughts. Inside a terrible pressure was building. An overpowering mental anguish whose cause I couldn't identify brought tears to my eyes.

At about two o'clock in the morning, unable to sleep, I decided to take a walk on the beach of Long Island Sound. It was a brilliant night. The moon was full and bright in a clear sky. The tide was up, and the usually calm sound was roiling in a frenzy. The sand trembled under the pounding of the waves. I was crying uncontrollably. With my ears filled with nature's fury and my mind filled with confusion, I cried out to the heavens, "I don't understand! I don't understand! I need to understand!" I begged God to release the unbearable pressure in my mind.

I don't know how long I stayed on the beach, but when I left my tension had lessened, and even the ocean and wind had calmed. As I walked back to my room, an unusual peace enveloped me. I lay in bed, wanting nothing more than sleep, but with a strange feeling of quietness. Then, over the course of a moment or so, something amazing happened.

My mind seemed to unfold. Thoughts that had been shrouded in darkness and confusion only a moment earlier were suddenly bright and clear. It was as if a veil had been lifted from my mind. Everything I had ever learned or read was available to me. Distant memories flooded back whole. I had the sense that I knew everything. I had only to direct my thoughts to a topic and the information would be there.

I was now wide awake and energized. All feeling of physical tiredness had left me. My mind was receiving information on any subject I cared to think about. It was like a sponge, soaking up information from the very atmosphere. My thoughts, previously fragmented and piecemeal, now were harmonious, complete. It was evident that something quite remarkable was happening. Was it my mind working like this? It felt so good, so right, yet I didn't understand. I had never thought like this before, but I was still me, wasn't I? I didn't sleep at all that night; I just lay in bed, waiting and wondering.

The next morning I was up at dawn. I dressed for class, not in the usual jeans and sneakers, but in slacks and shoes. I was anxious to learn. In class I sat in the front row, raised my hand, and became absorbed in the material. Information came quickly and was assimilated easily. After each class ended I would converse with my teachers for a better insight. I should add that these actions were highly uncharacteristic of me; I was not an intellectually aggressive student. I was still me, but now I seemed to be of two personalities. My old self hung around watching my new self explore its strengths. My mind felt like a precision machine running in high gear, and physically I felt great.

In my bright-burning state, I came to the unexpected conclusion that I was a genius. There seemed to be no other explanation for the elastic reach of my mind. Memory, logic, and the ability to integrate the two outdistanced all my previous experience. I had never given much thought to the definition of a genius, nor had I personally known anyone who was gifted. But the accessibility of knowledge and the ease with which it came into my hands seemed encompassable only by some notion of genius.

Holding to the logic that a genius cannot be wrong, it followed that everything I thought and did had to be right. For example, since I did not feel the need to eat, it was alright not to. I was not tired; why sleep? This state continued for about four days—four days of little or no food, and little or no sleep. I couldn't spare the time for such activities, nor could I have slept had I wished to. Physically I continued to feel great. I just couldn't shut down my mind—or body.

At the peak of intense activity and intense certitude, I started to make mistakes. I became confused. At work I tried to adjust the time clock so that I would not have to make my rounds every hour but could punch in all the rounds at once. I did so not out of any intent to deceive my employer but because I had lost the sense of what was appropriate on the job. My thoughts became mixed up and confused, coincident with the onset of exhaustion. Worse, the logic behind my self-identification as genius began to unravel. A genius should know everything, I thought, but now sudden gaps began appearing in the flow of information that only a few days before I had handled so easily. I didn't know everything, couldn't do everything, didn't understand everything.

I'm not a genius, I don't know everything. What's going on in my mind? Maybe I'm Jesus Christ. Yes!—No! That can't be, He was here already. Well, maybe I'm His little brother. Yes, that makes sense! I'm Jesus's brother . . . no, maybe not . . . I don't know. . . . These thoughts seem crazy now, but at the time they were as real as life itself.

The following day in class my confusion and physical exhaustion snowballed. My mind was out of control, grabbing any stray thought and running with it, then leaping to a different thought. These fragments seemed to be connected, but not in any way that I could discern. I argued with my instructors. I seemed to oscillate between a high level of intellectual functioning and irrationality. As my mind careened from fragment to fragment, from insight to irrationality, it seemed to occupy a completely different sphere from my body.

As the hours of this singular day wore on, the thought of being Jesus's brother impressed itself more and more heavily in my mind. It was not logical that I should be Jesus, but since I had had an older brother who had been killed, it seemed at least possible that I could be Jesus's brother. That much of the analogy was incontrovertibly in place.

I decided to research this question at the library. As I sat down with a half-dozen or so Bibles, my psychology teacher appeared. By then I was crying uncontrollably, saying over and over that the answers were in those books. My teacher knew something was wrong and had been looking for me. He took me to a school counselor, who in turn called my parents. Two hours later my mom and dad were driving me to the hospital.

My dad remained with me in the emergency room, which helped me stay calm. Beneath that facade, however, I was seething with agitation. I wanted to lash out or run. A man in a white lab coat approached me, probed me. He wanted to give me a shot. I felt confused again. I trusted my dad, but I didn't trust the man in the white coat. What to do, what to do? A memory of the movie, "One Flew Over the

Cuckoo's Nest," came to mind, accompanied by visions of mental institutions and lobotomies. Convinced that the doctors had tricked my dad into believing them, I nevertheless decided to let them give me a shot. My parents left shortly after I fell asleep, and I was alone.

I slept for a day and a half. When I awoke, my thoughts seemed to have slowed down. Over the next ten days the doctors tested and observed me. I told one of the attendants my thought about being Jesus Christ. His expression became so grave that I decided never to mention it again. I didn't want them to think I was crazy. I was diagnosed as manic-depressive, put on lithium, and released.

The apparent cause of my manic episode would later be charged, in part, to three traumas earlier in my life. The first was the death of my older brother, who had been killed in the fall of 1971 by a drunken driver. Three years later, in the fall of 1974, my best friend contracted an infection that left him confined to a wheelchair. The third incident came in the fall of 1977, when I was deemed ineligible to play college hockey. In retrospect, sports, especially hockey, had been my main source of comfort and release. Skating across the rink, caught up in the physicality of the moment, I was distracted from the ever-present pain in my life. Sports were the only way I knew to avoid the pain locked in my heart. With that crutch gone, it was only a matter of time before I would have to face my pain.

When I was released from the hospital I was told I would have to take lithium every day to prevent a recurrence of the mania. When I asked how long I would be on lithium, I was answered with a shrug and a look that suggested no one really knew the answer. I was given appointments to have my blood drawn every month to monitor the lithium levels, and also scheduled to see a psychiatrist. I went to the psychiatrist for several weeks, to no apparent effect. At age twenty-three I had no mechanism for reflecting on my life and did not consider I had anything to work out. And there was an additional fear: Simply going to the psychiatrist raised the specter that I might be crazy. I rejected that possibility utterly, and eventually rejected the psychiatrist as well.

I did, however, follow my doctor's orders religiously by taking lithium, 1200 mg a day, for four years. On lithium life seemed normal except in one respect: I had difficulty experiencing my emotions. Whenever I began to experience my emotions, began to truly feel them, I would go numb. Any strong feeling was cut off almost as soon as it came into being. Although this situation concerned me, I decided to let it be.

In the beginning I did not try to study my illness. I wasn't the doctor, just the patient. Like many others confronted with a frightening experience for which medical relief came promptly, I believed the doctor knew best. I turned over the responsibility of my experience to the medical profession. It would be another four years of a virtually emotionless state, four years of following medical orders, before I had enough courage to start reclaiming the whole of my life.

Explorations

S E C O N D   E P I S O D E

In the four years following my first experience of mania, my life outwardly resembled that of any other American college student's. I played hockey my senior year in college and graduated with a bachelor of science degree in criminal justice administration. During this time, however, I frequently found myself in libraries, searching through books on the functioning of the mind. I was not looking for a specific theory but for any information in any field that could help me understand what had happened to me. I wanted to know if other people had experienced or described aspects of the mind that might relate to my own experience. At the forefront of my quest was the pressing question, How could my mind have functioned at such a high level where memory and logic came together in harmony, and yet be considered abnormal?

An early book I came across was written in 1901 by Richard Maurice Bucke, a Canadian physician. Titled *Cosmic Consciousness*, this book explores the basis for a higher level of consciousness than the normal self-consciousness achieved by ordinary humans.

Bucke described three, increasingly comprehensive forms of consciousness:

1. Simple consciousness
2. Self-consciousness
3. Cosmic consciousness

Simple consciousness, in Bucke's construct, is possessed by the upper half of the animal world and is present when animals are conscious of things about themselves. *Self-consciousness*, which includes simple consciousness, starts when man becomes conscious of himself as an individual being separate from the rest of the world. *Cosmic consciousness*, which includes both simple consciousness and self-consciousness, is a state of understanding of life and the universe. The characteristics of cosmic consciousness include intellectual unfolding, moral elevation, a sense of immortality, and the understanding that life is eternal.

These characteristics of Bucke's cosmic consciousness come very close to the experience of the individual during mania. The intellectual enlightenment has its counterpart in the increase in memory and logical reasoning powers. The moral aspect correlates with the spiritual aspect, and the sense of immortality correlates with loss of the fear of death. The feeling of elation and the perception of the oneness of all things are common to both cosmic consciousness and the person experiencing mania.

According to Bucke, the origin of cosmic consciousness and of self-consciousness are very similar:

> The philosophy of the birth of cosmic consciousness in the individual is very similar to that of the birth of self-consciousness. The mind becomes overcrowded (as it were) with concepts and these are constantly becoming larger, more numerous, and more complex; some day (conditions being all favorable) the fusion, or what might be called the chemical union of several of them and of certain moral elements takes place; the result is an intuition and the establishment of the intuitional mind, or, in other words, cosmic consciousness.

In Bucke's conception, cosmic consciousness emerges in individuals over the gradual course of human evolution, and like anything else that evolves, it takes time to come to full fruition. At any moment in time or any period in history there exists a spectrum of forms of consciousness, a continuum, with individual minds occupying "all interme-diate planes between mere self-consciousness and the fullest cosmic consciousness."

Bucke used as examples of cosmic consciousness Buddha, Jesus, Saint Paul, Dante, Walt Whitman, Ralph Waldo Emerson, and Henry David Thoreau, among others. Although I did not place myself in the same category as these great minds, I began to see that a higher aspect of the mind has been realized in individuals throughout history. Moreover, as Bucke pointed out, every person who has expe-rienced cosmic consciousness has questioned the event with the thought, Is it possible that I may be going insane?

The question I ask myself now is, Is it possible that mania is somehow connected with the growth of conscious-ness? Could it constitute an intermediate plane between normal self-consciousness and cosmic self-consciousness?

In parallel with my readings, and wanting to pinpoint more exactly the nature of what has been called, over the centuries, "insanity," I began to try to work out for myself a basic structure of the human mind in relationship to the universe of all possible knowledge. I diagramed this struc-ture as three concentric circles, with the mind at the center and the universe of knowledge as the outermost circle, extending infinitely in all directions. As the universe of knowledge presses in on the mind, however, it encounters a filter in the intermediate circle. I pictured this filter as occupying the same place in relation to the mind as the moon's orbit around the earth. This filter limits the intake of information from the universe. It serves a protective func-tion, for it allows in only as much information as the mind can handle; it controls the flow of information. In mania, I see this filter as broken down or removed. The person expe-riencing mania is receiving so much unfiltered information that he or she cannot keep pace with it, nor does he or she know how to shut down the flow of information. An overload develops, and a short circuit will almost certainly result.

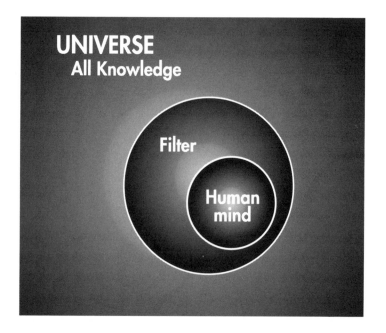

This structuration of the mind in relation to the universe of knowledge seemed a good beginning toward understanding my experience of mania, but it left many questions unanswered. What does the protective filter consist of? How is it broken down? Could such a filter be replaced with other, different filters that might allow access to more information? Does the mind itself create the filter, and if so, could the mind gradually loosen the protective bonds of the filter without injuring the biological being? Does removing the filter have to lead to mania? These questions occupied me from time to time, but at first I simply wanted to know if my idea about the mind and its protective filter was corroborated in what other people had said or experienced. Drawing a diagram of the mind was not an end in itself. It was a tool for helping me understand the condition called mania.

In reading in different areas, I had come across Aldous Huxley's *The Doors of Perception*. In this book Huxley documented his experiences with mescaline, believing that if he could change his normal mode of consciousness he might be able to discover what mediums, mystics, and visionaries were talking about.

Huxley drew on the work of the Cambridge philosopher C. D. Broad to explore the connections between the mind, memory, and perception. According to Broad,

> [T]he function of the brain and nervous system and sense organs is largely eliminative and not productive. Each person is at each moment capable of remembering all that has ever happened to him and of perceiving everything that is happening everywhere in the universe. The function of the brain and the nervous system is to protect us from being overwhelmed and confused by this mass of largely useless and irrelevant knowledge by shutting out most of what we should otherwise perceive or remember at any moment and leaving only that very small selection which is likely to be particularly useful.

This description was, I felt, the essence of my diagram. It also validated the recall ability that I experienced during mania as well as the feeling of being "overwhelmed and confused" by too much information.

Later Huxley quoted Broad as saying, "[The] mind at large has to be funneled through the reducing valve of the

15

brain and nervous system." Reading these words, I felt a thrill of excitement. The reducing valve in the biological system seemed to be a counterpart to the filter I had posited between the universe of knowledge and the individual mind. Could mania result from removal of the protecting filter?

TAKING CHARGE

To this point I had read widely other people's writings and experiences and had begun to formulate some ideas myself, but had not made any significant adjustments to my own life. The responsibility for my experience I had turned over to the medical profession. Medication and frequent clinic checks of my blood lithium levels kept me functioning more or less normally, allowed me to complete college and hold a job. I was not yet ready to re-integrate the two parts of my life, nor did I have sufficient knowledge of myself or my condition to do so. All this was to change radically with one striking incident.

In the fall of 1981 I was living and working in southern California. A friend invited me to Seattle for a brief vacation, a vacation that would become the turning point in my life. In Seattle I enrolled in a program for personal growth and development called Lifespring. The weeklong course provided individuals an opportunity to release stored-up emotions that had been suppressed for a long time. Although I was a little apprehensive about taking the course, I thought I would be fine as long as I continued taking lithium.

It did not take me long to release suppressed emotions. During the first day I found myself explaining to a group of strangers the intense sorrow and pain I had been carrying for ten years over the death of my brother. It was an incredible week. Each day we worked on another process. Emotions were brought to the surface, felt, then released. Anger, fear, love, hate, sorrow, laughter—it felt like a never-ending roller coaster ride. All the while I continued taking my medication, knowing that if I failed to do so I could be hospitalized.

As the program wound down, the overall theme centered on responsibility. Under the guidance of the instructor, we discussed the idea that every person is responsible for him-or herself. No one can sufficiently assume that responsibility for another person. Turning this idea into action, I began to take back my life.

Where does one start in assuming personal responsibility? I decided to start with the present, by learning everything I could about my illness and its medical treatment, lithium.

The following definitions are from the American Psychiatric Association's *Diagnostic and Statistical Manual of Mental Disorders, Third Edition,* revised (1987):

Manic Episode

The essential feature of a manic episode is a distinct period during which the predominant mood is either elevated or irritable, and there are associated symptoms of the manic syndrome. The disturbance is sufficiently severe to cause marked impairment in occupational functioning or in usual social activities or relationships with others, or to require hospitalization to prevent harm to self or others. The associated symptoms include inflated self-esteem or grandiosity (which may be delusional), decreased need for sleep, pressure of speech, flight of ideas, distractibility, increased involvement in goal-directed activity, psychomotor agitation, and excessive involvement in pleasurable activities which have a high potential for painful consequences that the person often does not recognize.

[. . .] Grandiose delusions involving a special relationship to God or some well-known figure from the political, religious, or entertainment world are common.

Another aspect of mania, called hypomania, is defined as follows:

Hypomanic Episode

The essential feature of a hypomanic episode is a distinct period in which the predominant mood is either elevated, expansive, or irritable and there are associated symptoms of the manic syndrome. By definition, the disturbance is not severe enough to cause marked impairment in social or occupational functioning or to require hospitalization (as required in the diagnosis of a manic episode). The associated features of hypomanic episodes are similar to those of a manic episode except that the delusions are never present and all other symptoms tend to be less severe than in manic episodes.

When I approached my experience from the medical point of view, it was clear that my thoughts and actions fell in the category of mania. But when I tried to find out more about what underlies mania, the information stopped. The rest is conjecture. Mania might represent a chemical reaction in the brain, or it might be an inherited trait. Others think that mania that first shows up in an adult could be a late result of a head trauma sustained during childhood. There is not much evidence to substantiate any of these theories, nor is the experience of mania itself well researched. If a person exhibits the symptoms of mania, then he or she is considered manic—the definition is circular. Treatment then entails drug therapy and a stay in a psychiatric treatment center. Although I do not see this approach as wrong, I do see it as very limited.

I next turned to the area of medication. Lithium, when introduced into psychiatry, met with great success in the treatment of the manic phase of manic-depression. Lithium is an element. It acts more like sodium than like any other ion. The use of lithium for mania came about in the 1940s, when J. F. Cade, a physician in Australia, used lithium salts experimentally in an attempt to increase the solubility of urates in guinea pigs, and noted that lithium produced catonic states in the guinea pigs. Jumping ahead, Cade administered lithium to manic patients and noticed that it had a beneficial effect on their symptoms. Lithium has since been noted to have several effects in the chemical transmitter systems believed to be involved in depression and mania. The known side effects include hand tremors, diarrhea, and nausea. In long-term use it has been associated with hypothyroidism. Here again, the interworkings of lithium with the human biological system are largely unknown.

With this information at hand, I tried to put together as many aspects of my experience as I could. Initially I focused narrowly on the "facts" of mania—the symptoms and their treatment. What struck me as interesting was that in the first few days of my mania—actually hypomania—I had stopped eating and sleeping. I wondered what would happen if a normal person in a normal state of awareness stopped eating and sleeping for four or five days. Would that person continue to function in a rational, coherent manner? People deprived of food and sleep usually become disoriented and cannot function in a consistent and reasonable way. What might have happened, I wondered, if the hospital that treated me had only put me to sleep, and then made sure that I ate a balanced diet, instead of putting me directly on lithium? Would my mind have slowed down to a reasonable functioning level? Or would I still be psychotic, unable to function? The next step in my explorations, I decided, would be an investigation of the role of food and sleep in maintaining health.

In my readings on diet and fitness, one idea seemed to be universal: You are what you eat. This idea was first formulated by Hippocrates, the Father of Medicine, in the fifth century of the pre-Christian era. In *Corpus Hippocraticum,* Hippocrates (or one of his followers) wrote,

[I]t appears to me necessary to every physician to be skilled in nature, and to strive to know, if he wishes to perform his duties, what man is in relation to the articles of food and drink, and to his other occupations, and what are the effects of each of them to everyone.

Hippocrates stressed the importance of knowing the effects of food and drink on the systems that make up the biological and spiritual entity known as man. He also stressed the interrelationships of eating and "other occupations" and the many different systems in the human body.

The brain is made of cells, just like the rest of the body, and will similarly react to various nutrients or toxins introduced in food. If we do not eat properly or observe our own reactions to certain foods, we will never understand how we function, either physically or mentally.

The idea that mental functions can be affected by substances taken into the body has been expressed by Dr. Marshall Mandell and Lynne Waller Scanlon, authors of *Dr. Mandell's 5-Day Allergy Relief System*. This book explores the role of various substances taken into the body in causing cerebral allergy. Since no actual causes have been credited for the onset of mania, I was interested in this book in a general way: for what it might tell me about the effects of food on the mind.

In the Foreword to *Dr. Mandell's 5-Day Allergy Relief System*, written by Dr. Abram Hoffer, Hoffer says,

> There is no doubt in my mind that certain people's brains react adversely to a variety of substances by becoming schizophrenic. If cerebral allergy can cause that most deadly of all mental diseases—schizophrenia—it can surely mimic all other conditions as well, such as learning and behavior disorders, depression, anxiety, etc., and it does.

Later in the book Mandell writes, "I have also provoked [with different food combinations] severe forms of mental illness, including paranoia, catatonia, schizophrenia, and *manic-depression*" [italics added].

With the information I had compiled, I decided that a diet change would be the most logical way to start taking responsibility for my life and the treatment of my condition. I became involved with a medically supervised program called Nutrionics which addresses metabolic management through computer technology. A series of laboratory analyses of urine, blood, and saliva are performed to determine trace metals and other chemical components in the body. The results are recorded in a computer program, which uncovers metabolic patterns that can serve as a guideline for determining a diet that will deliver optimal nutrition for the individual profiled. The data may also indicate the need for detoxification from certain dietary components, exercise, and vitamin and mineral supplementation. The results of my tests were quite startling. The computer printout read,

> The unbalanced left pattern of the patient would suggest either diabetic, pre-diabetic, or dysinsulinism tendencies. These patterns exhibit great mood swings. Refined carbohydrates should be strictly avoided but complex carbohydrates are essential.

I was counseled that eating simple sugars would make it hard for me to maintain my emotions on an even keel. Instead, I was to eat complex carbohydrates regularly. With this information, along with other information I had garnered from my reading, I was prepared to take some concrete steps toward improving my health.

I began with a seven-day fast intended to cleanse my body of built-up toxins. Although fasting was totally foreign to me, information I had collected indicated it was both logical and safe. In conjunction with fasting, I also underwent colonic irrigation.

The Nutrionics program encouraged meditation and exercise along with dietary changes as part of the total program for enhancing health. Body and mind seem to need opportunities to reduce stress and tension. To that end I began to take forty minutes a day, twenty minutes in the morning and again in the evening, when I would just sit quietly and let the worries of the day roll out of my consciousness. I also used music occasionally so that my mind would have only one stimulus, the music, instead of many distracting thoughts. For exercise, I mapped out a jogging course and set a timetable to follow.

The seven-day fast started slowly. I seemed always to be hungry. Not until the fourth day did my body feel comfortable, and then the last three days went quickly. I fasted with two other people who were also learning about the ways food affects the body. Together we formed a strong support group, each looking out for the others.

When the fast ended the new diet began. I started slowly, first by removing all foods with preservatives and chemical additives. Then I replaced carbonated beverages with water and juice. In the first few weeks on the new diet I lost twenty pounds and my energy level increased noticeably.

With my diet reset on a healthier course and with a regular schedule of exercise and meditation in place, I faced an important question: Should I stop taking lithium? When I was released from the hospital four years earlier, I was cautioned that if I failed to take lithium I would have another manic episode. Going off lithium would test my theories on the relationship of diet and rest to mania. Did I have enough faith in myself that I could do this? I was scared, and rightly so. Without lithium, I feared the onset of mania. Would my new controls work? Would diet, meditation, exercise, rest, and a supportive environment be sufficient to quell the power of mania? When I considered the worst possible outcome—if I was wrong, and if mania was an illness, at worst I would end up back in the hospital— things did not look so bad. I made my choice and stopped taking lithium. What I could potentially find out about myself was worth the risk.

The first couple of days were exciting. My feelings of well-being soared. The feeling of freedom was tremendous, but the fear in the back of my mind was just as strong. Then I began to experience some of the same phenomena as during my manic episode four years earlier. My memory increased and my logical powers blossomed. My brain absorbed information as though it were a dry sponge set in a bowl of water. My physical energy increased dramatically. In my state of heightened awareness, I was unusually percipient of other people's thoughts and attitudes; I was able to "read" them. I do not mean that I could read their minds or know in advance what they were going to say. Rather, I was receiving enough information through all my senses that I could feel the direction of their conversation.

Intellectually, I felt alert and curious. My mind raced with thoughts and ideas. Information streamed into my consciousness like running water. As before, my appetite left and my need for sleep diminished. But the difference this time was that I had anticipated these changes and was prepared for them. I forced myself to eat every day, and I continued meditating so that my mind could slow down and rest. I would put myself to bed, and although I was not able to sleep for a full eight hours, I did sleep a few hours each night.

Early in this second episode of hypomania—for that is what it was—I put together a comprehensive physical fitness program for a friend with amazing insight and speed. I felt as if I could accomplish anything. My mind gave me ideas and information at a rate that astounded me. As during my first experience, I could actually sit back and watch my mind work with swiftness and precision; it was as if I had two minds. I was enthusiastic about everything. There was not enough time in the day to do everything I wanted to do. I also found it frustrating to have to wait for anything to happen. People around me seemed to be going about their work in slow motion.

The enthusiasm and high mental achievement had, however, a darker underside. I began to feel great pain and remorse over the waste of my life. For the first time in my life, I realized that I could have anything I wanted; all I had to do was reach out and take it. Why had I not been able to tap into these extraordinary mental powers except when I was manic? As I became absorbed in these thoughts, anger, fear and frustration welled up inside me. One evening, as I tried desperately to think of ways to correct my past and recover my dreams, I was overcome by anxiety and panic. Finally I lay down and rested until I fell asleep. When I awoke in the morning things seemed more in perspective, and most of the pain had left me.

This phase lasted six to eight weeks. By Christmas my mind had slowed down to a normal level of functioning. I stayed on my new diet, improving it whenever I could. It seemed that I did not need lithium. My controls of diet, sleep, and relaxation had worked as well as or better than lithium. In this, my second experience of mania, although my mind functioned at a far higher level and far more efficiently than I had ever thought within my capability, I did not lose control or become disoriented. I wanted to know why. I had faced the dragon and won, but what had I won?

Toward a Definition of Mania

I had now had two radically different experiences of mania. In both instances, however, my mind exhibited extraordinary powers I had never thought possible, especially in relation to myself. The only thing I wanted to do was figure out exactly what had happened to my mind. It was at this time that I set my life's goal—to fully understand the workings of my mind. As I repeated this statement over to myself I thought it unrealistic. Who in his right mind would do such a thing? It was certainly not the normal career goal of the eighties. But however strange it sounded, it felt right.

How does one go about investigating the workings of his own mind? I decided to start with the question, What is mania?

The definition of mania is elusive. To the medical profession mania is abnormal, a "disease" that needs to be cured, or at least curbed, with lithium therapy. Yet Dr. Ronald P. Fieve in his book *Moodswing,* offers a different perspective on mania:

> [M]any forms of manic elation seem to be a genetic endowment of the same order as perfect pitch, a photographic memory, great intelligence, or artistic talent of any sort. Manics not only have fabulous energy when they're not too manic, but a qualitatively different, quicker, more perceptive grasp of others and their surroundings.

Still working within the medical or biological framework of genetics, Dr. Fieve suggests that mania at the same time stands outside this framework. Medical terms are simply insufficient to explain mania.

Yet a third view proposes that mania is somehow tied in to a higher level of consciousness. Could mania be an opening to this higher consciousness? Its effects certainly suggest enhanced intellectual functioning, with greater recall ability, logical reasoning, and sensitivity to surroundings. Reading more books on the higher realms of the mind, I was to find that there is no one definition of higher consciousness, let alone instructions on how to achieve that state. There seems to be a question of sanity involved in the experience of a "psychic awakening." As well, systems of thought that propose a higher level of consciousness usually tie it in to an advanced spiritual state. So I could see my path taking a slight shift toward the spiritual aspects of consciousness.

In looking for a definition of mania, I found myself with more questions than answers. Was mania a gift that simply needed to be understood? Was mania a religious experience? Did appropriate therapy simply help people experiencing mania maintain their behavior within the constraints dictated by the needs of their body? I had maintained control over my mind during mania when I carefully fed and rested my body. And while I was doing this, my mind worked at a level I did not believe possible. What if mania is the way our minds are supposed to work? Scientists tell us that humans use only a tiny fraction of our minds living and working, and this fractional use is considered normal. Could mania be the release of a greater part of the mind for use? At some future time, might people regularly be able to think and perform at fifty, sixty, or even one hundred percent of their capacity without becoming manic?

These questions came from deep inside me. It was difficult for me to sort them out. I felt as if I knew something I could not explain. I felt as if I were involved in a game whose rules no one knew.

The education I received looking for answers over the next few years amazed me. There seemed to be no one correct explanation of mania. I read books on Islam, Buddhism, Christianity, and many other religions, looked into the writings of Einstein, Plato, Socrates, Freud, and Jung, visited practitioners of the occult arts, took workshops on intuition and psychic powers. Throughout, I kept looking to others to help me get to a place where only I could go. In a sense, my education during these years simply readied me to do something I had to do for myself.

MORE WORK

One item mentioned frequently in my research and with which I had had some personal experience was meditation. Meditation has been used throughout human existence as a way to relax and clear the mind. I had successfully used meditation as a control during my second experience of mania. I would sit quietly and try not to think of anything. As thoughts presented themselves to my consciousness, I would ignore them until I felt at peace. But what exactly was meditation doing to my mind? I decided to turn my attention to this area and learn as much as I could.

Meditation has been incorporated into many different philosophies, and many books have been written about it. The actual method differs with each philosophy. After reading a few books and practicing some approaches on my own, I decided to find a teacher. My first encounter was in a Zen monastery. I stopped in one day and found out the monks would lead me through meditation in exchange for work. This was fine for a Saturday, but I was looking for something I could do daily on my own time without having to exchange more time for work. I simply did not have enough time for both meditation and work. I thought I would talk to the head monk and explain my experience to see if he could help me, but when his secretary asked me why I wanted to see him, I changed my mind. I did not know how to explain my interest, and I did not want to sound like a crazy person. I left feeling confused and frustrated and decided to look around for another method.

I settled on transcendental meditation, or TM. I had read about TM, but the book I read did not go into the theory or methods of TM in any detail. Actually, it said you had to experience TM, because reading an explanation of it wasn't enough. There was a TM center only a half-hour from my house, so I drove over and signed up. It seemed to be a well-structured system. You gave them four hundred dollars, they gave you a mantra. A mantra is a spiritual word or phrase that is repeated over and over during meditation. Although four hundred dollars seemed steep, I knew that education was not free. And in a way, learning a method to control my mind would be my true schooling.

For the next few nights, I practiced my mantra and learned more about TM. I was taught not to resist my incoming thoughts but to let them in and follow them until they stopped or ran into one another. This felt better than my earlier exercises in meditation, for it provided more of a flow and less resistance to thoughts. As the babble of thoughts died away on its own, the mantra would resurface. I continued my new meditation practice every day, twice a day, until it was automatic. I came to look forward to these times and felt very relaxed and centered when finished.

I had now two different approaches arranged in my life, diet and meditation. As I acquired some experience with meditation, I continued to make alterations in my diet.

After removing foods with preservatives and chemical additives I eliminated red meat, canned foods, refined sugars, and some dairy products. I investigated the relationship of food to human biology and mental functioning, and tried out some of the ideas in my own diet. One idea was a rotation diet, in which you do not eat the same food within a four-day period so that you can determine if you have a reaction to any kind of food. I also tried food combinations, in which certain foods were always eaten with other foods and some foods were never eaten together. These differences allowed me to experience various aspects of conscious eating. This seemed a step forward, for instead of focusing on the negative aspects of eating certain foods I was focusing on the benefits, and also creating a more interesting diet for myself.

Changing my diet was not difficult when I was in Seattle and in the company of other people who were also eating as I was. When I returned home to New York, I did not have as much support in choosing a healthier diet. I was involved in learning how humans as a species are directly and indirectly affected by the foods we eat, and it took me a while to find people who shared my interest. The lack of immediate social support also meant that time and effort had to be given to the selection and preparation of new food choices. Meditation also became difficult to keep consistent. The time and space needed for meditation were not always readily available.

Whenever a person changes his or her way of living, there is always a certain resistance within the individual that causes stress. The better prepared one is for change, the easier it will become. That is why being in a supportive environment when one makes fundamental changes to one's life will always be beneficial.

A House Divided/ The Subjective vs. Objective Mind

Over time I had amassed a wealth of information on higher states of the mind, body, and spirit as these states are incorporated into different systems of thought. Often the information led to new insights, but equally often it was contradictory. In an effort to sort out this information and perhaps find general relationships between different systems, I put together a chart of higher states (see page 38). Although simple, it gave me a point of reference. In this chart I lined up four kinds of systems, or four approaches, that seemed to have stages in common. The occult view comes from Rudolf Steiner, founder of the Waldorf Schools. (The Waldorf Schools seek to balance the arts and sciences, with an emphasis on the development of moral and objective thinking, as an aid to nurturing and understanding the full human experience.) The religious view is embodied in the three temptations of Christ. The approach of philosophy comes from the work of Carl Jung, and the medical view reflects the present-day medical understanding of mania. Depending on the view one adopts, each system has a truth in its own right.

As the chart suggests, throughout history man has been described as a trinity of body, mind, and spirit. Development of the individual at each level is predicated on development at the immediately preceding level: Development of the mind is based on development in the physical plane of existence and in turn prepares the way for spiritual development. The test of adequate functioning at each level is whether the individual can remain within the broad parameters of the level during development. If functioning is inadequate, confusion can result. The confusion or inadequacy will be exposed in the trial, the temptation, or inflation.

Higher States in Different Systems

	Occult	Religion	Philosophy	Medicine
Body Level 1	Fire trial	First temptation	Superiority complex	Increased awareness
Mind Level 2	Water trial	Second temptation	Inflation	Identify with genius
Spirit Level 3	Air trial	Third temptation	Megalomania	Identify with God
Result	Initiation	Born again	Re-centering	Ignorance
	Higher wisdom	Son of God	Individualization	Insanity

What I needed most at this time, however, was not a comparative chart but a frame that would encompass all of my experiences and ideas. I found such a structure in the work of Dr. Thomas Jay Hudson, a remarkable man who lived in the mid- to late 1800s. Hudson was an attorney and journalist who spent his adult life in Port Heron, Ohio, and died in 1903. He was also an inventor, a politician, and fascinated by the mind. His ability to express in words the workings of the mind made him a leader in the field of psychic phenomena. Hudson made extensive reference to hypnotism in his work. Hypnotism was a widely accepted method of investigating the mind before the advent of Freud's "talking therapy." The terms of hypnosis—suggestion and control—infiltrate Hudson's writings and probably were instrumental in helping him develop his view of the mind.

In *The Law of Psychic Phenomena,* published in 1893, Hudson outlined a structure of the mind that I have found invaluable in understanding the experience of mania. Hudson saw the mind as having a dual character, which he described as the subjective mind and the objective mind. The properties of the dual mind are as follows:

The objective mind takes cognizance of the objective world. Its media of observation are the five senses. It is the outgrowth of man's physical necessities. It is his guide in his struggle with his material environment. Its highest function is that of reasoning.

The subjective mind takes cognizance of its environment by means independent of the physical senses. It perceives by intuition. It is the seat of the emotions, and the storehouse of memory. It performs its highest functions when the objective senses are in abeyance.

Suspension of the objective mind, the objective senses, is most easily achieved in a dreamlike or hypnotic state. That may be another reason why Hudson referred to hypnosis in his studies—to better expose the functions and powers of the subjective mind.

The objective mind sorts incoming information from the world and uses it to construct a reality framework. The objective mind cannot be controlled by the suggestions of another if those suggestions run contrary to the objective mind's knowledge of the world. The subjective mind, on the other hand, is immediately and always open to the power of suggestion. This is especially so when the guiding compass of the objective mind has been removed, as during hypnosis. In Hudson's words,

[T]he subjective mind [of a hypnotized individual] accepts, without hesitation or doubt, every statement that is made to it, no matter how absurd or incongruous or contrary to the objective experience of the individual. If a [hypnotized] subject is told that he is a dog, he will instantly accept the suggestion, and to the limit of physical possibility, act the part suggested . . . . If he is told that he is in the presence of angels, he will be profoundly moved to acts of devotion. If the presence of devils is suggested, his terror will be instant, and painful to behold.

Importantly, the subjective mind of an individual is susceptible to the control of the objective mind of that individual, just as it can be controlled by the objective mind of another, as demonstrated in hypnosis. In other respects, however, the two minds have independent powers and separate functions.

Can an individual become aware of the separate functions of the two minds? In both of my experiences I had been able to sit back and watch my mind functioning at a superior level. I had the sensation of being a passive observer. Awareness of the separate functions of the two minds probably originates in the orderly, rational objective mind, so at some level I had that objective knowledge. But I had no way to accept or integrate the separate functions of the two minds. I lacked even an intellectual construct to help me understand that the mind might function in broadly different ways at different times.

I had also noticed, during mania, a sudden increase in my ability to follow logical reasoning to distant, fine conclusions. This is consistent with Hudson's analysis of the dual character of the mind, for Hudson saw the two parts of the mind as reasoning differently: "The objective mind is capable of reasoning by all methods—inductive and deductive, analytic and synthetic"—but the subjective mind "is incapable of inductive reasoning." Hudson appears to have followed the standard dictionary definitions of deduction and induction: To deduce is to infer from a general principle, to induce is to infer from particulars. In other words, deductions move from a general principle to the particulars that logically follow from that principle, whereas induction reasons from particulars to reach a general principle.

The deductive reasoning of the subjective mind is key to understanding the psychotic phase of mania. (Mania is now generally understood to manifest in three, progressive stages: hypomania, mania, and psychosis, with psychosis the most severe expression. If the mania is adequately treated, it need not progress to psychosis.) The psychotic individual relates to the world with his subjective mind only. Because of inability of the objective mind to retain control, he has no understanding of what is real or imaginary, so that any thought perceived is accepted as reality. The individual will accept any thought as the truth and will act and think from this premise (he is living a dream). And although a manic's thoughts may be bizarre and unusual, they are always logically sound.

Referring to the proposition, "The subjective mind is incapable of inductive reasoning," Hudson elaborated as follows:

The subjective mind never classifies a series of known facts, and reasons from them up to general principles; but, given a general principle to start with, it will reason deductively from that down to all legitimate inferences, with a marvelous cogency and power. Place a man of intelligence and cultivation in the hypnotic state, and give him a premise, say in the form of a statement of a general principle of philosophy, and no matter what may have been his opinions in his normal condition, he will unhesitatingly, in obedience to the power of suggestion, assume the correctness of the proposition; and if given the opportunity to discuss the question, will proceed to deduce therefrom the details of a whole system of philosophy. Every conclusion will be so clearly and logically deducible from the major premise, and withal so plausible and consistent, that the listener will almost forget that the premise was assumed.

To these two features of the subjective mind—a high degree of suggestibility and an exclusively deductive method of reasoning—Hudson added a third, perfect memory. Perfect memory seems to accord with the experiential aspect of the subjective mind. In almost all investigations of the mind, memory has proved one of the most astonishing and mysterious phenomena. In operations on the brain, for example, in the awake patient, when certain areas of the brain are touched the patient is able to recall a long-forgotten memory as if he or she were experiencing the remembered event for the first time. The existence of perfect memory, intact if profoundly suppressed in some deep layer of the mind, has long been hypothesized. Because science cannot locate or prove beyond all doubt the existence of perfect memory, it remains in the realm of theory. In any event,

Hudson regarded perfect memory, if it should ever be achievable, as a function of the natural operations of the mind and not at all abnormal:

> When we remember that the subjective mind does record, and does have at its command, all the experiences of the individual, and that, under certain abnormal conditions, in obedience to the initial impulse of suggestion, all its treasures are instantly available . . . we may rest assured that the phenomena displayed are the results of the operations of natural law.

If the subjective mind and the objective mind enjoy different powers, with the subjective mind under the control of the objective mind, the interesting question arises as to how the objective mind, in the natural order of things, should have come to this position of prominence. After reminding his readers that a house divided against itself cannot stand, Hudson noted the usefulness of having a single "controlling power in every well-regulated household, municipality, nation, or organism." Because humans live in a physical universe and carry out mundane acts of survival in relation to that universe, it seems appropriate that the objective mind, which reviews, sorts, and analyzes data about the physical world, should act as the regulator. If the subjective mind were to dominate the objective mind, the individual could not function in the physical world. Hudson suggested that anyone wanting to see the subjective mind in a controlling position should just visit a madhouse.

Hudson regarded the objective/subjective duality of the mind as of a kind with opposing, complementary forces observable everywhere in the universe: "There is a positive and negative force in the greatest physical power known to mankind. There is a male and a female element in every race and order of created organisms. . . ." Yin and yang. When the opposing forces of the mind are perfectly balanced, working in synchrony, the result is genius. Hudson understood genius as a normal condition that is achieved through the natural operations of the mind, even if it is achieved rarely or only for very short periods at a time: "True genius is undoubtedly the result of the synchronous action of the two minds, neither predominating or usurping the powers and functions of the other." But he particularly cautioned against giving the subjective mind free rein: "When the subjective is allowed to dominate, the resultant acts of the individual are denominated 'the eccentricities of genius.' When the subjective usurps complete control, the individual goes insane." The figure on page 45 shows the dominance or synchrony of the objective and subjective mind in relation to normal mental functioning, psychosis, and genius.

Hudson's work provided a coherent foundation I could use to start piecing together my own experience of mania. Mania, in fact, fits exactly Hudson's description of a dual mind. Mania reflects the subjective mind's powerful urge to present itself to the objective mind, while the objective mind sits back and watches the extraordinary display of the subjective mind. Phenomenologically, this is the start of hypomania. The objective self is somewhat in awe of the hitherto unknown powers of the subjective mind and goes along blindly, all the while trying to sort out the experience in a rational way. Mundane things, the sole responsibility of the objective mind, are overcome by the sheer force of the subjective mind and are casually tossed aside. Eating and sleeping are the first mundane activities to be discarded.

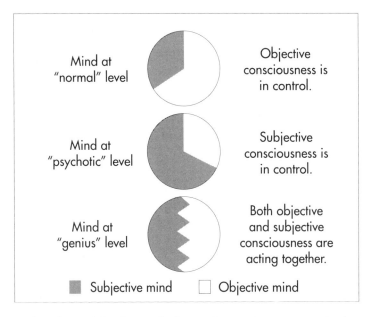

As the subjective mind continues its ascent during mania, its powers, particularly memory recall and deductive reasoning, are more and more in evidence, usurping the logical, rational tastes of the objective mind. Other, more particularized expressions of the subjective mind also become evident when it is operating on this area of its curve. These expressions are taken up in the next chapter, which places some of the more exotic but consistently observed behaviors of manic people within the framework of the dual mind.

CHAPTER 5

God, Sex, and Energy

In case histories of mania, certain claims and behaviors are repeatedly documented:

- The manic claims to be a genius.
- The manic person aligns him- or herself with Jesus Christ or some other deity.
- The fear of death disappears.
- The manic person becomes sexually aggressive.

These features, so universal as to be diagnostic of the state of mania, typically occur in a behavioral matrix of high energy and high enthusiasm. The word enthusiasm comes from the Greek word *enthos,* meaning "the god within." The origin of the term suggests that the enthusiastic person is in touch with the godlike powers of creation and the potential for universal knowledge. But, as Norman Vincent Peale noted in his book, *Enthusiasm Makes the Difference,* enthusiasm is a tricky thing: "[E]nthusiasm builds a fire within a person, but he must control his enthusiasm for an idea or a project rather than be controlled by it." Peale suggested that enthusiasm should always be tempered by judgment and reason, for "uncontrolled enthusiasm can destroy, just as controlled enthusiasm can create."

Peale's understanding of enthusiasm seemed analogous to what I had read of the powers of the subjective mind as they are manifested during mania. And just as enthusiasm must be tempered by reason, so that the individual can direct his enthusiasm in a constructive manner, so the powers of the subjective mind as they are expressed during mania must somehow take direction from the objective mind. Many of the customary behaviors of a manic person can be explained by the subjective mind operating under insufficient guidance from the objective mind. In fact, all of the manic behaviors and beliefs listed at the beginning of this chapter seem to be manifestations of the overwhelming dominance of the subjective mind.

The manic claims to be a genius. In the last chapter we looked at Hudson's concept of genius as emerging from the perfect synchrony of the objective mind and the subjective mind working together. In mania, eventually the subjective mind overpowers the objective mind, and the perfect harmony needed for genius is lost. But for a brief period the manic does experience the phenomenological rudiments of genius and is aware of it. The manic person will always question the validity of the experience, for he or she knew that his or her mind did not work in this fashion previously. Moreover, genius is only recognized by others over time, if it is recognized at all. Thus, both societal validation of genius and the manic's previous life experience will cast doubt on the claim to genius. But the lack of validation does not mean that the mind is not working in a genius-like way during mania. Also, the language for discussing genius is not readily available. If a person claims to be a genius, it is easier to label that person crazy than to try to find out what he is experiencing.

In my first episode of mania I did have the experience of genius, in Hudson's sense. Moreover, I believed I was a genius, and as my subjective mind with its deductive reasoning powers took over, certain conclusions flowed logically from that premise. But I had made one bad mistake in the premise. Never having studied or thought much about genius, I assumed that a genius was someone who knew how to do everything. As time went on, it became painfully clear that I did not know how to do everything; therefore, I could not be a genius. But what else could explain what was happening to my mind, if not genius? The dissonance between what I expected a genius to do and my actual experience of genius in Hudson's sense, which I now feel is the correct understanding of genius, was too much for me. This dissonance probably aggravated the confusion and mental pressure I felt and may have hastened the events that led to hospitalization.

The manic person aligns him- or herself with Jesus Christ or some other deity. I was not a genius; was I Jesus Christ? My logical reasoning said no, because Jesus had already lived on earth, and died. Was I Jesus's younger brother? I had experienced the death of my older brother, so logically this idea seemed to have some merit. For reasons I am unaware of, the element of time did not come into play—Jesus had lived two thousand years ago, so being His younger brother would be unrealistic—but it should be noted that the subjective mind does not seem to operate within linear time. In any event I did not accept being Jesus's younger brother as a fact, only a possibility.

Because I was functioning from deep within my subjective mind, I now wonder whether I could have been in touch with my own immortality and therefore reasoned out the possibility of being God. This conclusion would be in keeping with the logical deductive powers of the subjective mind, operating unchecked by the inductive reasoning of the objective mind: If all men are mortal and only God is immortal, then a person who believes himself immortal must also be God, or a god. Is this why the fear of death disappears in someone experiencing mania?

The point I am trying to make is this: Man enfolds within himself the mortal and the divine. Both aspects are always available, but we usually operate within the parameters of the mortal, objective universe. During mania, the links to the divine suddenly come into view with the ascent of the unfettered subjective mind; Hudson forthrightly referred to the subjective mind as the "soul." The manic person, operating from the subjective mind, will feel the sudden release and awareness of the soul.

The fear of death disappears. In *Cosmic Consciousness,* Richard Bucke stated that one of the characteristics of the cosmic sense is the individual's loss of the fear of death. The individual comprehends that some aspect of the self does not pass away with the physical death of the body. He or she sees the body as the vehicle of the soul. The soul itself is part of the universality of all things and cannot be extinguished.

The characteristics of cosmic consciousness resemble what is experienced during mania. Or, to turn this statement around, the manic person experiences the enlightenment of cosmic consciousness. There is the same intellectual and psychic enlightenment, increased recall ability, a feeling of elation, and a belief in personal immortality. Importantly, during mania the individual perceives hitherto concealed relationships: He or she sees the oneness of all things. This same perception is held by the nonmanic person who has achieved cosmic consciousness. At this point, during mania, the subjective mind kicks in, adding the logical conclusion that a person who is immortal must be God.

The manic person becomes sexually aggressive. While in the hypomanic state I was very aggressive sexually. I appeared to have dropped most if not all of my inhibitions. When my psychology instructor found me in the library and put me in touch with a female counselor, I did everything I knew to seduce her. The majority of women with whom I came in contact while in a manic state I made advances toward. The medical profession describes this situation as loss of inhibition, and seems to find the description adequate for its purposes. I was interested in what underlay the loss of inhibitions, and particularly the loss of sexual inhibition and the appearance of seduction displays.

In his discussion of the dual mind, Thomas Hudson listed three primary functions of the subjective mind: (1) preservation of [the individual's] life, (2) the instinct of reproduction, and (3) preservation of human life in general. The second function of the subjective mind, the instinct of reproduction, sheds some light on the promiscuity of the manic person: He is following a basic instinct of the human species. As the subjective mind ascends to prominence during mania, the expression of this instinct is pushed into the foreground. It is all the more noticeable if the objective mind, which reasons out the consequences and appropriateness of actions within dominant social codes, is not operating in harmony with the subjective mind. The strictures surrounding sexual expression in society are very rigorous and tend to highlight any variation.

Richard Bucke's characterization of cosmic consciousness offers a way out of this impasse. Bucke emphasized that moral elevation is part and parcel of the experience of illumination. Most religions incorporate celibacy for their novitiates during training for the spiritual life. Rudolph Steiner in *Knowledge of the Higher World and Its Attainment* also states that it is essential that the student of a higher spiritual life should strive for a moral character of absolute purity. Now, mania seems to offer one path, if a difficult one, to the experience of illumination. Unless the person who is experiencing mania has been sufficiently grounded in moral conduct, the instinct of reproduction will express itself forcibly, unchecked by any control. Even with training, enforcing these controls takes time and constant effort. During mania, somehow the subjective mind must assimilate and accept the guidance of the objective mind in expressing the instinct for reproduction. And an individual cannot begin to provide the necessary guidance unless he or she is aware of the two different minds, each with its own powers and functions, that must be integrated.

All of my experiences during mania, and the behavior of other manic people as recorded in case histories, fit beautifully into Hudson's framework of the dual mind. The ability to recall, the lack of concern for eating and sleeping, promiscuity, the marvelous deductive reasoning power, the phenomenological experience of genius, and a belief in immortality all are explained by the actions of the subjective and the objective mind, either working in synchrony or in opposition to each other. Of greatest interest was the revelation of the powers of the subjective mind, and the potential for the two minds to work together, each nurturing the other. The subjective mind and the objective mind must be perfectly balanced in order for humans to function at their highest intellectual and spiritual level. This high level of functioning occasionally becomes available during mania. And with the information I have gathered I am convinced that mania, although potentially highly dangerous to the person experiencing it, is one of the greatest gifts the human race has ever received.

THE PROBLEM OF LANGUAGE

One of the most difficult problems I have encountered in my quest to understand mania and the functions of the human mind has been a problem with language. Some words have a different meaning for every person who uses them. God, soul, and mind are just three terms that vary from book to book and person to person. I started with God.

Because I am Catholic, God to me means God the Father, God the Son, and God the Holy Ghost. The next step was to determine, What is God? After years of searching and asking questions, I finally came up with a workable definition that not only feels right to me but is in line with the teachings of many different religions. I define God as total energy, both manifested and unmanifested energy. I was taught that God is everywhere and manifested in everything; this definition includes both these aspects. I was also taught that God is immortal. Because energy cannot be destroyed, it can only change form, its eternal existence correlates with the immortality of God.

Working from the definition of God as total energy, I arrived at the following syllogism: If God is all energy in the universe and man is a manifestation of energy, then man is God.

The words of the Scripture bear out the divinity of man. The following passage is from John 11:33:

> The Jews replied, "We would not stone You for a good act but for blasphemy, because You, a human being, make yourself God." Jesus answered them, "Is it not written in your Law, 'I said, you are all gods'?"

How can modern-day humans experience the divinity of God, as related in Jesus's words? Abraham Maslow (d. 1970), the founder of humanistic psychology, helps us toward this goal in *The Further Reaches of Human Nature,* published posthumously in 1971, Maslow wrote,

> Transcendence also means to become divine or godlike, to go beyond the merely human. But one must be careful here not

to make anything extrahuman or supernatural out of this kind of statement. I am thinking of using the word "metahuman" or "B-human" in order to stress that this becoming very high or divine or godlike is part of human nature even though it is not often seen in fact. It is still a potentiality of human nature.

As Maslow pointed out, there is the danger that an individual will believe he is THE God. Although it seems to be a paradox, it can be understood by an analogy. If you fill a pail with ocean water, the pail contains the ocean water with all of its characteristics, but at the same time it is not the ocean. The physical body is not unlike the pail. It is a limited structure of energy that contains the characteristics of energy but is not all energy.

I now found myself with an interesting predicament. If I am god but not God, and if the subjective mind only reasons deductively, then I must believe myself to be god in order to be complete. It took time to understand and feel comfortable with this idea. Is it right to strive to be god? Saying that I wanted to be god not only sounded a bit crazy, there was also the chance that striving for this logical but preposterous goal could be dangerous. Not only might it be iniquitous, it could also lead to another psychotic episode. Yet I had to take the chance of being wrong. My curiosity was stronger than my trepidations. I decided I wanted to be god.

Striving to be god has a venerable history. *The Corpus Hermeticum,* written thousands of years ago, underlines the need to be godlike in order to understand the nature of God. Hermes Trismegistus ("thrice-great Hermes"), to whom the work is attributed, was the legendary author of works incorporating mystical, philosophical, and alchemical doctrines; the ancient Greeks identified him with Thoth, the Egyptian god of wisdom. His teachings were followed by the

Gnostics, a religious cult of the late pre-Christian and early Christian eras that held that enlightenment comes through knowledge of spiritual truth. The following passage is from *The Corpus Hermeticum*:

> Unless you make yourself equal to God, you cannot understand God; for the like is not intelligible save to the like. Make yourself grow to a greatness beyond measure, by a bound free yourself from the body; raise yourself above all time, become Eternity; then you will understand God. Believe that nothing is impossible for you, think yourself immortal and capable of understanding all, all arts, all sciences, the nature of every living being. Mount higher than the highest height; descend lower than the lowest depth. Draw into yourself all sensations of everything created, fire and water, dry and moist, imagine that you are everywhere, on earth, in the sea, in the sky, that you are not yet born, old, dead, beyond death. If you embrace in your thought all things at once, times, places, substances, qualities, quantities, you may understand God.

Many others throughout the history of mankind have either thought of being God or realized that in some form or another they were indeed God, so the idea of being God is not new. The three writings I have quoted in this section—the Bible, Abraham Maslow's work, and *The Corpus Hermeticum*—support the divinity of man from, respectively, a religious, a psychological, and a historical point of view. But to openly suggest, in this day and age, that you can both strive for and attain this spiritual goal will bring down upon you the wrath of the Church and the questioning of your sanity. So I decided to keep my conclusion and direction to myself.

ENERGY IN ACTION

My path had now taken a distinct shift in the spiritual direction. In order to continue proceeding in this direction, I decided I would need some practical experience in balancing the objective mind with the subjective mind. Remembering that many of Thomas Hudson's insights into the mind came from thinking about hypnosis, I felt this would be something useful for me to try. I went to a hypnotist and read on my own about self-hypnosis. Hypnosis is a state of heightened suggestibility in which an individual is receptive to ideas and suggestions from himself or someone else. The person who is hypnotized is always aware of what is going on.

While experimenting with self-hypnosis I had two interesting experiences. The first came after the third day of practice. As I lay in bed giving myself suggestions, I felt my head turn to the right and then to the left, but my physical body did not move. I then sat up, although I did not move physically, and proceeded to drift down the stairs and into the kitchen. That was my first out-of-body experience.

The following day I had a second experience. As I again lay in bed giving myself suggestions, I felt myself float down what appeared to be a distance of an inch, stop, float down another inch, and stop again. This happened a third and a fourth time. On stopping the fourth time, however, I found myself elsewhere: sitting in the sun on top of a ridge overlooking a harbor. The sky was the most astonishing color of blue I had ever seen. Not only could I see color, which I had never been able to do in dreams or visualizations, I could also feel the sun's heat on my shoulders. All during this experience I kept reminding myself not to move in the bed, lest I end the experience.

I do not know how long the experience lasted, but I remember coming out of it the same way I went in, one level at a time, until I came back to my room and opened my eyes. I was ecstatic, jumping around the room. I wanted to understand what had happened but did not know whom to ask or even who would believe me. After that experience I never went back to hypnosis; I just let it go.

I began finding some answers a month or so later when I enrolled in a course in psychic phenomena that was taught at the local community college. The course examined human energy fields and basic psychic phenomena such as astral travel and auras. The first experience I had had was explained as a common first step in astral travel: the individual has the sense of the head turning to the right and left, although the body never moves. My second experience was also explained as a somewhat more complex and prolonged out-of-body experience.

The course instructor was very interesting. He had the ability to produce an energy field, an aura, that most people in the class were able to see as a glowing, dull yellow energy pattern surrounding his body. Although I had heard of the existence of auras, I had never before seen one.

In later classes we were taught how to access the healing power of our own auras by means of visualization meditation. In this form of meditation the healer wills the flow of energy from the healing level of his aura down through the throat chakra and out through the heart chakra. A chakra is a power center of the body; there are seven major ones. The energy is visualized as a flow of color moving through the chakras. It can also be visualized as moving out of your body and into someone else's. Because the supply of energy in the aura is infinite, it can be drawn on indefinitely through the chakras. There is always more energy if you know how to access it.

The healing that I performed happened during the third week of class. A friend had stopped by to see me. She seemed to be a little depressed and tired. As we sat and talked, I felt as if she were pulling my energy away from me. I felt a definite discharge, a dimming of my own energy levels. I started to pull back from her, first mentally and then physically by turning away. Then I remembered what we had been taught about transferring energy, and I reversed tactics: instead of pulling back, I opened up. I took my friend's hand in mine and focused my eyes on hers. Then I mentally performed the visualization exercise, all without her knowledge.

The change was immediate and astonishing. Her eyes became brighter, full of life. Her depression left, and her energy level increased noticeably. For my part, I had a completely new experience. I could actually feel an energy transfer. I felt a physical drain as I opened up my heart chakra; and then, as I visualized more energy flowing in from my aura, I felt its presence and movement flowing through me. This lasted about two or three moments. As the pull of energy from me slackened, I continued my own pull on my aural energy until I felt replenished.

After my friend left, I considered what had taken place. I knew what had happened physically: I felt it. I knew what had happened mentally: I thought it. But I didn't know exactly what had happened. When I described my experience to the instructor during the next class, I was informed that the energy transfer that took place was called an energy healing.

Soon after this course was over I enrolled in an intensive five-day course called "Intuition and Psychic Development."

The course consisted of different exercises intended to help individuals access their latent psychic abilities. During the course we would perform various meditations and mental exercises that would allow us to become more sensitive to the world around us and to trust our own intuitions. It was these exercises, some of which I continued on my own outside of class, that triggered my third manic episode.

Third Episode

◎

"Intuition and Psychic Development" was taught by a
woman who was said to have the ability to access other people's thoughts. Although I was somewhat skeptical of this
claim, after the first day I was convinced that she could, to
a very high degree, access the thoughts of other people. The
first couple of days of class we discussed the different ways
in which the mind works and began to form a comfortable,
supportive group. It was on the third day of class that my
third round with mania started.

During class on the third day the instructor paired everyone with another person to form partners for the day. The
exercise consisted of deep breathing in conjunction with
different kinds of music played at different volumes. Each
couple decided which partner would do the exercise first,
while the other partner would be available for support; then
the partners would switch roles. This exercise was very
much like the exercises I had done several years earlier with
Lifespring, in that breathing and music were involved. The
use of music to move the mind beyond its immediate concerns seems to be a constant element in awareness-enhanc-
ing work. Thomas Jay Hudson in *The Law of Psychic
Phenomena* observed that music is "one of the most potent
means of inducing the subjective condition." At the time,
however, I was unaware that I might be putting myself in
danger by accessing the subjective mind without adequate
control by the objective mind.

As we continued to breathe with the music, we were
instructed to let our minds relax and express anything that
came up, whether the expression was oral or by way of physical gestures. At the end of this exercise we were allowed to
lie down and rest. My experience literally exhausted me. I
felt as if I had run several miles and now needed desperately to sleep.

After class ended I went home and went straight to bed. As I lay in bed trying to sleep, my mind felt as if it had been struck by a mallet. Then, just as had happened during my previous experiences with mania, I felt my mind expanding as though it were a dry sponge that had been set into a bowl of water. I repeated the thought, "I am psychic, I am psychic," over and over out loud. My physical exhaustion left me. I was completely energized and awake.

The next thought that crossed my mind was that it was my birthday and Christmas at the same time (it was neither). At the time I was staying by myself in the apartment of my girlfriend, who was away for a few days. I proceeded to search the entire apartment for my presents, which must have been collected over the years and stored there without anyone's knowledge. I also remember thinking that I had lived ages and ages ago and had come back at this time, and all the things I had cherished in the past were to be found in the apartment. I spent the rest of the night tearing the apartment apart. By morning the place looked as if it had been ransacked by thieves.

Class the next day was very exciting. We did an exercise in which we cleared our minds of all thoughts and then focused on another person, trying to pick up any information, which we would then relate back to that person. We worked in groups of four, with three people concentrating on the fourth. A woman in my group asked if there was anything she could do to help her three-year-old daughter. As we concentrated on her, I had a sensation of joy, and as I was informing her of it the thought of an elevator came to mind, although I could not tell why. Another person in the group looked at me and said that the woman's daughter was in the elevator. At that moment the elevator door opened at our floor and the woman's husband and daughter stepped out.

They had come by earlier than planned to pick her up. Although I was not sure what was happening, I am convinced, from this and similar experiences, that there is a wealth of information about our being that we are blind to.

On the train going home that night I decided to try an experiment. I wanted to see if I could create a mental disturbance by yelling silently in my mind while directing the vibration toward the passengers seated in the train. As I stood at the front of the car facing the passengers, I noticed that many were sleeping or reading. I felt strange trying to psychically yell at everyone, but it was only for fun, and besides, it might not work. So I gave a mental yell, focusing the mental vibration toward the passengers. I was shocked. About seventy percent of the people looked directly toward me, making eye contact. I wanted to leave. I felt a tremendous sensation of pressure, as if everyone were upset with me. I broke off the eye contact and looked down at the floor, smiling to myself and saying, "I don't believe this but it worked."

The following days were exciting. I was in a heightened state of awareness, and it felt great. Any time I wanted to know more about anything, I had only to focus my mind on the subject and the information would come. I seemed to be able to access my subjective mind at will. When I released my attention, I would not receive any more information. This frightened me a little. I was also afraid that I would lose this ability, so I called it back time and again just to reassure myself that it was still there.

When the class ended, on Friday, I decided to take a weekend trip to the ocean. En route I stopped off at an art gallery that sold paintings by local artists. As I viewed the paintings with my subjective mind, they seemed to come to life. I felt as if I were in the artist's soul. I seemed to be able to see through their eyes, feel their emotions. Anger, love, loneliness just flowed out of the paintings.

This state continued for another day or so, but it was fated not to last. I had slept poorly or not at all for several days. Driving back home from the ocean, I went through several emotional cycles. I was experiencing feelings that had been suppressed for years. As each came to the surface on its own, I would act out whatever I felt. Major release work was going on that seemed to have no end.

I awoke Monday morning with the thought that I was a wizard. I was not sure where this thought came from, but, in keeping with my exercises, I played the part. Eventually I came to believe that not only was I a wizard, I was a "wizard's wizard"—the best of the best. I seemed to be losing touch with reality while still able to function in the physical world. In fact, I seemed to be operating at the intersection of three different worlds. One was the mystical world, in which I was a wizard and could access other people's thoughts. One was the linear world, the normal everyday world in which we live. And one was a magical world where I saw all the people in the world playing the parts of characters in Alice in Wonderland, caught in the trap of their own ignorance. I had a vision in which I held in my hand the missing pawn from the chess game that represented the world. I was floating from one reality to another, never knowing how or why I got from one to the next.

This merging of realities started to become dangerous. I was on the road, trying to get home, when, for unknown reasons, I stopped my truck in the middle of a three-lane highway, got out, and walked over to the side of the road. As I stepped in front of a car going sixty miles an hour, then quickly jumped back, I remember chastising myself, "You're not God yet!" A truck had pulled up on the side of the highway. I jumped onto the running board and asked the person sitting inside if he knew who I was. I was thinking he was supposed to follow me because I knew where to go. To put it mildly, he did not know who I was and could not have cared less. He told me to get off the truck before I got hurt. I took his advice and headed for my truck. As I glanced around I noticed a vagabond picking through a garbage can. As I watched this man I perceived that he and I were one. The duality, the separation into two beings, existed only in the physical forms, which I knew and felt were illusion.

I got back into my truck and set out for home again. I never made it. While driving homeward, I felt/saw two small explosions of white light in the middle of my head that nearly made me drive off the road. I was desperately trying to get home, but my world was falling apart. My imagination started to run wild with thoughts of some evil force that was preventing me from getting home. The paranoia came crashing in. I was caught in an evil vortex, defined by the major highways in the area. I had to get off the highway before it was too late. But how? The answer came that everything was backward. Following out this premise, I put on my left blinker and exited right. As I approached the traffic light, I drove in the left lane to make a right-hand turn, cutting over at the last moment.

I turned down onto a side street. As I left the evil vortex of the highway behind, my energy faded completely. My eyes started to close. I slowed the truck to five miles an hour and slowly crossed the double yellow line. Everything seemed to happen in slow motion. The thought now entered my mind that everything was alright, that God would go as slow as He had to so that I would have time to understand. I struck another vehicle, causing minor damage. Then my truck rolled onto the shoulder, knocking down a sign before coming to a stop.

Sitting in my truck, agonizing over my condition, I started to cry. I felt disorganized and beyond hope. I seemed to be thinking normally one moment and in the next I felt lost—psychically, emotionally, profoundly lost. I had gone too far. I would not be able to stay sane. I would never get home. I had a crushing sense of failure. In complete frustration, I screamed out to the universe: "I can't do this anymore! I can't do this!" In the ensuing silence, out of nowhere, a voice said, "Yes, you can. You can do this." The voice radiated love and joy, so much so that I felt centered and calm. I looked around to see who had spoken, but there was no one there. I heard those words as clearly as I hear the words I speak, but I did not understand where they came from.

The police showed up, inevitably, and I was taken by ambulance to the nearest hospital. I was caught. I had not escaped the evil vortex. I was obsessed by the thought of evil. I imagined that the medical center was the power center for evil and that the police and some of the staff were also evil. Those staff who were not evil did not realize that they were working in an evil place. As I was wheeled into the emergency room, two thoughts arose in my mind. The first was triggered by the sight of an elderly gray-haired woman who was being wheeled down the hall to a different area. I immediately saw her as Helen Keller, and at the top of my lungs I screamed out her name: "Helen! Helen!" And the second thought was that now everyone had heard me scream, so the evil forces would have a harder time getting rid of me. The more people who heard me, the safer I would be.

I was tied to the gurney and a blood sample was taken from my arm. I was admitted to the psychiatric ward but left in the emergency room. The doctor ordered the attendants to give me something to eat, and requested another blood sample. As I looked around I saw a calendar behind the nurses' desk that had fairies on it. This was comforting, for it gave me the feeling of being watched over.

At this time there was a shift change and two different nurses came on duty. They were both blond and dressed in green hospital garb. I recognized these nurses as my protecting fairies in the flesh, but I also understood that they could not tell me because it would endanger them. So much evil! My mind seemed to jump from a magical level back to the linear level. I had no control over it.

I had to get out of the place. I needed to find the key. What was the key? The ring! That was the key. Earlier in the day I had taken a ring from my girlfriend's apartment because I thought someone else would like it. I was now convinced that this ring would make me invisible, and once I was invisible, I could escape. My "normal," objective mind was telling me I had totally lost it. My subjective mind was saying, "Trust me. This will work." And: "You'll never know unless you try."

I asked to go to the bathroom. Because I had been very calm for a while, the staff agreed to untie me. In the bathroom I slipped the ring on my finger, all the while watching myself in the mirror. Nothing happened. Can an invisible person see himself in the mirror? I wondered. This is crazy, it's not going to work. Yes, it will work, if you believe. I took a deep breath, opened the door, and walked out of the room and down the hall. Nobody stopped me! It's working, I am invisible. I walked out of the hospital and into the woods across the street. I had found the key, the ring worked.

I stayed in the woods for a while until my mind switched back to the linear state. I knew that the police had my truck, and that the hospital personnel were probably looking for me. If I did not return I would be in trouble. So I walked back into the hospital. They asked me where I had been. I told them I had just stepped outside for some air. I wanted to go home, but the doctor told me that I had already been admitted and that I would have to talk to the psychiatrist on duty because he was the only one who could release me.

The psychiatrist's office was on the other side of the hospital. I was escorted there by two attendants through a maze of tunnels. The paranoia was coming on again. The only way I could keep the magical and sinister forces in balance was to keep on talking to the two attendants. When we finally reached the psychiatrist's office I was told it would be against hospital policy to release me. I insisted that I was fine and should go home. The psychiatrist brought in a colleague, and together they questioned me. Finally, to my relief and surprise, they agreed to release me, provided that someone came to the hospital and picked me up. I telephoned my brother Jim, who took me home.

That night I could not sleep. My body seemed to be burning up. I tried a cold shower, but that brought only temporary relief. I felt very religious and wrapped myself in a multicolored blanket—a "coat of many colors." I sat in front of a bureau that to my mind was actually an altar, and meditated. I was concerned to know how many levels of experience there were. I could identify three—linear, magical, and mystical—but I believed there had to be more. I asked my family, but no one knew. My family realized that something out of the ordinary was going on and decided to take me to the local hospital for an evaluation.

At the hospital I started to feel paranoid again. I attacked my sister Debbie, who was trying to help me. The police officer wanted to handcuff me. I begged my brothers not to let him do it. As the office came toward me with the handcuffs, Mark, my younger brother stopped him in his tracks, telling the officer that he and his brothers would take care of me. I calmed down enough to let the nurse give me a shot of thorazine, which would help me sleep. The local hospital would not admit me and instead sent me to a psychiatric center in the next town.

I was in the psychiatric center for almost two days before I woke up. I think they were even worried that I had been given too much thorazine. I was put on lithium and Haldol during my stay in the hospital. I kept a journal of how I was feeling each day. I asked to see the *Physicians' Desk Reference* so that I could look up Haldol. It was described as a major tranquilizer used in the management of psychotic disorders, although its mechanism of action was not established. I noticed that my vision seemed always blurred and that I was unable to concentrate for any length of time. I tried to show my journal to my doctor, but she refused to look at it or even discuss lowering the dosage of Haldol. I had the feeling that not too many patients ever questioned her or kept a journal. An interne working with the doctor did, however, take the time to read my notes and was able to persuade the doctor to lower the dosage of Haldol I was receiving.

After fourteen days I was released from the hospital. I was put back on lithium and warned that if I went off it, I would have another manic episode and end up back in the hospital. I was also told to join a support group run by the hospital so that I could be watched.

What happened? Where did I go wrong? Seven years of research and personal work went down the drain. To find out what had happened and why, I had to piece the puzzle together myself.

Why did I lose control? To start with, I did not keep track of my sleep, nor did I maintain a constant food intake. I also did not take the time to meditate. I had let my three major controls falter, and so I had no way to rest or direct my mind. I was also able to pinpoint another kind of control that would be useful. In my second experience I was very focused. I channeled every thought I had into devising a physical fitness program, whereas in my first and third episodes I had no focus whatsoever. I just went anywhere my mind decided to go.

As everyone knows, mistakes sometimes provide more knowledge than successes. My third episode was triggered by the exercises in the course I was taking, but in some ways I had allowed myself to drift into a situation in which mania could occur. I had not bothered with the physical controls as I had before. I was caught off guard, and I paid the price. But I learned something new. I learned that I must cultivate my ability to focus and concentrate. I could not allow myself to be swept away by every thought and emotion that crossed my mind whenever I experienced a heightened state.

And there was the problem of lithium to deal with again. As soon as I got out of the hospital and had time to reflect on where I had gone wrong, I ran right up against the medical approach to controlling mania. I really felt that lithium was not the answer. In my second episode it was not lithium that kept me functioning, it was the controls of diet, rest, and meditation. So, without telling anyone, I again decided to stop taking lithium. I renewed my meditation practice and watched what I ate. Nothing untoward happened. My mind did not start to open. I just went on functioning at the "normal" level of consciousness.

CHAPTER 7

Concentration, Imagination, and Will

My third episode taught me that concentration is key to maintaining control over the mind during mania. In the beginning stages of mania, actually hypomania, the encounter with the subjective mind is so overwhelming that the individual's ability to control his response in a mature, judicious manner is decimated. In my first experience with mania, I was unable to concentrate on my thoughts. My mind jumped from one thought to another, one reality to another, in scattershot fashion. I was able to understand this erratic behavior when I reviewed my second experience. During my second experience I was focused on developing a physical fitness program. All my energies, thoughts, and actions were directed toward one idea. I was totally concentrated, and I achieved that concentration because I had set my mind to a particular goal. I had used my will, defined by Webster's as the power to choose what one will do, or determination. Both focus and will were lacking during my first experience. It seems that these two elements, will and concentration, are tools to be understood and used if a person wants to have control over the powers of the mind.

In my third episode I again lacked concentration. Although I knew I was losing touch with reality, I could not force my subjective mind back under the control of my objective mind for any length of time. I was able to keep a grip on my mind for brief periods by talking to the hospital attendants. My thoughts and energies were channeled into the enormous rigor of holding a rational conversation. But that was only a temporary expedient, and as soon as I loosened my grip or lost focus—in other words, as soon as I stopped talking—the paranoia came crashing in again. I found it impossible to sustain the effort that was needed to keep my subjective mind from taking control.

As my mind wandered between realities in my third episode, a new kind of reality had opportunity to intrude and make itself known. My mind ran with thoughts of wizards, magical rings, fairies, and evil. The intrusion of the world of magic seemed related to my lack of concentration. When my concentration slackened, fairies and evil returned. But where did these thoughts come from? I decided they came from the imagination. Now, imagination is usually thought of as good: beneficial, creative, productive. But it seems that imagination when not subjected to any control can be destructive. I wanted to see how concentration, will, and imagination might work together to keep the mind in balance; or, contrarily, how they might run amok in the state of mania.

CONCENTRATION

Everyone seems to know intuitively what concentration is. We say we are concentrating on a book, or a project, or a person, or that we are no longer concentrating on something and can shift our attention elsewhere. But to achieve a mode of concentration, other than by trial-and-error learning, is not easy. Concentration is not simple, in concept or in practice.

In *The Power of Concentration,* published in 1918, Theron Q. Dumont provided twenty lessons designed to strengthen the individual's power of concentration. To develop concentration, Dumont advised, you must begin by observing your own actions, both your mental thoughts and your physical movements. All actions, whether mental or physical, are manifestations of the mind. Dumont put it this way: "As the mind is, so is the action. If it is uneasy, restless, erratic, unsteady, its actions are the same. When it is composed, the mind is composed. Concentration means control of the mind and body. You cannot secure control over one without the other."

As you learn to observe both your thoughts and your actions, you begin to develop more than just the power of concentration. Just as you are what you eat, so you also are what you think. Thoughts in fact mold your life; they are the source of your actions. And just as thoughts may be destructive or constructive, so they can direct your life in negative or positive ways.

Here is the first sounding of a theme that Dumont returned to repeatedly: Concentration is not an end but a tool to an end. As a tool it can be used well or used poorly. Its immediate end is control, but there are other ends, more important, that similarly enfold control as a tool. As a tool, concentration is applied in actions that mold the mind. The ultimate goal is self-knowledge, which in turn hones the mind for more action. To start over, concentration, by improving control, brings the mind into readiness for more work.

In Dumont's description of concentration, I began to see similarities with another area in which I already had experience, meditation. The following passage seems to be a call to meditation:

You will find that the man who concentrates is well poised, whereas the man who allows his mind to wander is easily upset. When in this state wisdom does not pass from the subconscious storehouse into the consciousness. There must be mental quiet before the two consciousnesses can work in harmony. When you are able to concentrate you have peace of mind.

Mental quiet or silence is the goal of meditation. The process of meditation involves sitting still, watching your physical actions, and watching your thought processes without intentionally thinking. That is also the process that develops concentration. Meditation focuses the mind by freeing the objective mind from its distractions and allowing it to approach synchrony with the subjective mind—a correlation with the two consciousnesses working together in harmony, mentioned in the quotation.

Dumont mentioned a danger that could arise in developing concentration: it may become involuntary concentration. Involuntary concentration occurs when the thoughts an individual has been focusing on become so locked in the consciousness that the individual is always thinking of them. This happens when you bring home problems from work instead of leaving them at the office. Thoughts become the master of you instead of you being the master of your thoughts.

Dumont also identified three reasons for the inability to concentrate:

1. "Deficiency of the motor centers"
2. "An impulsive or emotional mind"
3. "An untrained mind"

Of these three reasons, the first, a deficiency of the motor centers, is the hardest to correct because it involves willpower. Dumont understood deficiency of the motor centers as being related to underdevelopment of the autonomic faculties of the brain. He defined willpower as mental energy that is gathered together and focused on one point. The will, in Dumont's conception, is an overarcing principle by which an individual can control his moods and circumstances instead of being controlled by them. It is through the development of the will, the focus of concentration, that a person is able to choose his own fate.

In Dumont's conception, will and concentration are related through what he called an active force. This force operates in every individual, but it is strongest in the person who is aware of it and knows how to use it. It is

> that "force" that makes us feel determined at times to do something worth while. It is not thought, emotion, or feeling. This driving force is something distinct from thought or emotion. It is a quality of the soul and therefore it has a consciousness all its own. It is the "I will do" of the will. It is the force that makes the will concentrate. . . . This driving force is within us all, but until you reach a certain stage you do not become aware of it. It is most useful to the worthy. It springs up naturally without any thought of training. It comes unprovoked and leaves unnoticed. Just what this force is we do not know, but we do know that it is what intensifies the will in demanding just and harmonious action.

Could this active force be housed in the subjective mind? Or is it something else, something unknown, that directs and controls the subjective mind?

The will is also related to desire. In fact, desire seems to be the springboard for the will. Out of desire comes the focused attention that leads to concentration, that allows an individual to direct his action to something of ultimate interest rather than to things of immediate interest. Into desire go feelings and emotions—all the highly subjective elements that uniquely compose an individual's psychic makeup. "Desire," Dumont wrote, "is the motive power that imparts the energy to action. The will is more like a guiding, directing force which applies the energy of the desire." And: "Desire is the evolved stage of Feeling and Emotion. It is the link between Emotion on one side, and Will on the other side."

At this point I constructed a hierarchy of the elements in Dumont's work as they relate to the structure of the mind. At the bottom of the hierarchy is desire, which is nourished by feeling. ("Feeling guards the very outer gate of knowledge," Dumont wrote, "and determines largely what shall or shall not enter therein.") Feeling provides the orientation and attitudes of desire. Desire is energy. At the intermediate rung is will, which gives shape to the energy of desire and is also itself a form of energy. Will can be strengthened by practice, and is not evident until it is put into action. At the top of the ladder, and knitting together all the lower layers, is an "active force." This force drives the will to action.

This scheme can be rephrased in simpler terms. Our feelings and emotional states create our desires, which in turn affect our will. The will follows the strongest desire at any moment. Desire is the preface to all subsequent action; it is the Great Motivator.

Concentration stands slightly to the side of this hierarchy of relationships. It is a tool that focuses the energies of desire and will, transforming them, step by step, into action. The action it leads to is the proper use of knowledge—in the long run, to achieve self-knowledge and self-mastery. Knowledge alone is not enough, just as the tool of concentration is not enough. Both must be used, and used appropriately, to achieve a goal selected by the individual.

IMAGINATION

What part does imagination play in the scheme of things? Why was I under the assumption that I was a wizard's wizard? That I was trapped in an evil vortex, or protected by fairies, or had a magical ring? Theron Dumont addressed the subject of imagination in another book, *The Master Mind*. Dumont understood imagination as closely related to memory, but not it exactly: "Memory reproduces only the original impressions placed within its realm, while imagination reproduces the recorded impressions of Memory, not in their original condition, but in new groupings, arrangements, forms. . . . [Imagination] never makes new materials."

Imagination, then, is a tool that uses the material supplied by the memory to create new ideas and avenues for expression. But imagination is also subject to misuse. It is misused when it is not directed toward a goal, when it is allowed random expression in the form of "idle day dreams and vain fanciful flights of the imagination," in Dumont's words. Not all daydreams and fancies are improper, of course. They become nonprofitable only when they are habitually moved into the position that action should rightfully occupy. And the goal of action or work, in Dumont's construct, is knowledge, particularly self-knowledge, which in turns bears fruit in more action.

Imagination can be used constructively to advance us toward a goal in a decisive manner. Dumont stated that it is necessary to direct the power of imagination into one's own work: character building and self-mastery. Within these guidelines imagination can be directed and used as an active creative force.

Imagination, then, like concentration, is a tool to be used by the individual to advance his or her knowledge. Used properly, it is a powerful constructive tool. But if accessed without meaningful desire and control (willpower), it can become a powerful destructive force. An analogy can be drawn with fire. Fire is a powerful tool that is used well when used with knowledge and skill, but when used carelessly it can become dangerous to the point of death. Just as powerful as fire in the physical world is imagination in the mental world, and if carelessly used it may similarly become a destructive force.

WILL

After I finished the two books by Dumont, I drew a rough diagram of the forces and energies that can be used on the path to self-realization (see page 85). A short time later, while browsing in a bookstore, I came across a book titled *The Act of Will,* by Roberto Assagioli. The cover design was a diagram that, although in another form, was identical in its conceptual organization to my diagram.

Roberto Assagioli was a colleague of Jung and Maslow and a pioneer of the Italian psychoanalytic school. He developed the concept of "psychosynthesis," which holds that humans evolve naturally toward a state of harmony within themselves. Assagioli saw the will as playing a major role in human growth. In *The Act of Will,* Assagioli listed seven qualities of the will, assigning two or more descriptors to each category. The seven categories are:

1. Energy (dynamic power, intensity)
2. Mastery (control, discipline)

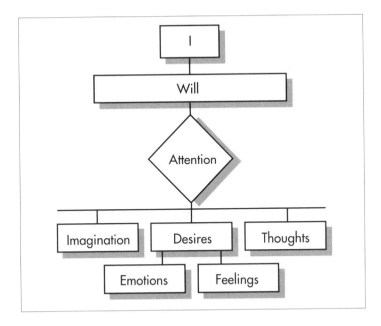

3. Concentration (one-pointedness, attention, focus)
4. Determination (decisiveness, resolution, prompt-
   ness)
5. Persistence (endurance, patience)
6. Initiative (courage, daring)
7. Organization (integration, synthesis)

Although these qualities of the will at first glance seem
unnecessarily complicated, with some thought we can see
most if not all of these characteristics already at work in our
own lives. The will is a tool, and like any tool it has properties and limits. Knowledge of these properties and limits
allows us to choose whether or not to use the will, and when
we do use it, to do so with mastery. By dissecting the will
into its separate characteristics we can begin to identify
which characteristics are strongest in our personal lives and

which are weak. We can then improve our conscious control of our own will and so use the will more effectively as a tool. Assagioli also listed six stages of the will. They are:

1. Purpose
2. Deliberation
3. Decision
4. Affirmation
5. Planning
6. Direction of the execution

Again, the purpose of breaking down the will into its component stages is to better understand the will and be able to use it more effectively. An individual reflecting on these stages of the will might find, for example, that the second stage, deliberation, receives little attention in his personal life. He is then able to focus on this underpowered stage and increase his facility in using the tool of the will.

To this point we have considered what might be called personal will. The application of personal will in our daily lives helps us achieve certain goals we have set for ourselves. The will also operates much more broadly in the human experience, ultimately linking the purposeful life with the anima of the universe. Assagioli developed this idea by discriminating two other kinds of will. One is the transpersonal will, the other is the universal will. Transpersonal will is the will that directs the individual to align his activities with the highest aspects of his being. Transpersonal will supercedes personal will but ideally works in harmony with it. Universal will is part of a universal reality, that aspect of "oneness" that religions throughout time have alluded to. The universal reality is beyond the individual's grasp, yet the individual is part of it. Our intellectual understanding of universal oneness relies on analogy: As microcosm is to macrocosm, so our individual reality is to the universal reality.

Transpersonal Will

Transpersonal will, often latent in man, makes itself known as the force behind the quest for meaning. Why do we exist? What is our purpose in life?

The transpersonal will comes from the transpersonal self, the highest aspect of man. It is the aspect of man that transcends the limiting personal consciousness without losing awareness of its own individuality. We can see this aspect of the self come into being in the "hierarchy of needs" outlined by Abraham Maslow in his book *Motivation and Personality*. As the basic psychological needs of the individual are met, the personal needs next clamor for attention. Among the personal needs are the need for love, for belonging, for esteem, and for self-actualization. When these personal needs are fulfilled, the door is open for the expression of the transpersonal self. The transpersonal self is expressed through the transpersonal will, which, Assagioli wrote, "operates from the superconscious levels of the psyche. It is its action which is felt by the personal self, or 'I,' as a 'pull' or 'call'." It is this aspect of transcendence, when the individual aligns him- or herself with transcendent values, that Maslow referred to as "metahuman" or "B-human."

The metahuman experience is still part of the human potential; it is not something separate from and above the human condition. Moreover, the hierarchy of needs does not have to be completely satisfied at each step in order for the transpersonal will to make itself known. Although the different stages in development are distinct, they are not separate. All stages can coexist in the same person at the same time, with some stages so undeveloped as to be practically nonexistent while other stages may be highly developed. Thus, according to Assagioli, "one can have achieved a certain measure of genuine transpersonal self-realization while not having complete self-actualization." Complete self-actualization requires that all the needs of the different stages in the hierarchy of needs be satisfactorily met.

Universal Will

Assagioli admitted to difficulty in approaching the subject of "universal will" because for many years it was in the province of religion. Nevertheless, he wrote, "The existence of a universal mind, of an inherent rationality of the Universe, has been affirmed by many in various ways, both philosophical and scientific."

Assagioli understood the universal will as a sort of ultimate reality in which all things are related through correspondences or analogies—likenesses. As microcosm mirrors macrocosm, so there is a close correspondence between man and universe. These likenesses and correspondences exist in an essential unity that is the fabric of the ultimate reality in which everything participates.

The universal will, the sense that we are all one, has been noted throughout time. It is the Tao of the East, the "Father" of Christianity. Yet, as Assagioli noted, identity in nature does not mean that man in his social environment or in his normal state of consciousness is fully participating in the essential unity, or even understands it. As part of nature, man has within himself the requisite ingredients to experience universal oneness; yet this oneness, even as it surrounds us and infiltrates our being, stands somewhat "above" us. It is something we must strive to attain.

My investigation of the will took me, by degrees, back to the realm of God. All the philosophical systems I have read about start with the self and expand outward to a polar point that is itself of infinite dimension: God, total energy; and most philosophical systems suggest that humans are constantly evolving toward that pole of infinitude, or at least have the potential to do so. That potential is in each and every one of us. Each of us individually is capable of reaching a higher state. Sometimes the higher state is briefly revealed to us accidentally or as a gift, as during mania; more frequently it is reached by hard and thoughtful work. The highest way of being, or perfect self-realization, is sometimes called, for lack of a better term, the divinity of man. The divinity of man is just that: It is divine, absolute, godlike, but it is also the fullest expression of human potential. It is perhaps the most human of all human characteristics.

One fear that has constantly been with me in my search for truth has been the fear that I might be in denial. Almost everyone who experiences mania eventually tries to deny that the experience is an illness and tries to make it out to be something else. Denial is so general, in fact, that it has been incorporated into the definition of the illness. I had to wonder if my reading and searching were simply sophisticated forms of denial. Was I simply exhibiting a well-documented characteristic of the illness? I needed time to sort things out, perhaps time away from books.

My reading did suggest an interesting tack. I noticed that individuals have repeatedly sought out periods of solitude in nature—to be alone? To fast? I often wondered about the possibilities of this act and whether I, too, might benefit from spending an extended period of time in nature. Although I had never backpacked before, I decided to choose a trail that would allow me time in the woods. I picked the Appalachian Trail. This trail runs from Maine to Georgia, a distance of over two thousand miles, and takes approximately six months to complete. Hikers doing the full trail usually start at the southern terminus, in Georgia, to avoid the snowmelt of northern New England. On May 21, 1987, I stepped onto the trail and began a journey that has continued to provide material for reflection and learning long after the physical event itself melted into the past.

On the Trail

All great spiritual people down through time have sought solitude in nature. Was it just to be alone? It is not necessary to seclude oneself in nature in order to be alone. Nature has another gift to offer to those who seek it out, a gift that is seldom mentioned but always available. That is the gift of "pure reflection."

Modern psychology tells us that in most human interactions with other humans, what each of us experiences is only those feelings and emotions that we carry with us, and that our perceptions of other people really mirror how we think about ourselves. When we do not like what we see in ourselves, we project our inner state outward onto another human being, blaming the other instead of using our own dissatisfaction as a tool for self-reflection and personal growth. By going into nature alone, we seek out a mirror that we cannot shift our inner states onto. Because nature just is, and does not try to control or influence human life, every thought, feeling, and emotion is produced from within our own mental world. We are then forced to live in the moment and deal with what is.

Two thousand miles is shorter on paper than on foot. I needed to hike a certain distance each day in order to complete my journey before winter arrived in Maine, the northern end of the Appalachian Trail. I had a limited amount of time—determined by nature—within which to complete my journey. But within that single constraint of time I had ample and unexpected opportunities to make several discoveries about myself and the world.

I had no hiking experience when I started walking the Appalachian Trail. My backpack was an old pack that I had used as a suitcase on various occasions. When I filled the pack with what I thought were the bare necessities, it weighed seventy-five pounds. It was heavy but did not seem uncarriable.

The first day I covered three miles and became painfully aware that the pack was too heavy. As I set up camp that night, I found that a jar of honey had opened and honey covered every item in the food bag. After cleaning up this sticky mess, I proceeded to cook dinner. When I opened a can of beans with my knife the knife closed, pinching and cutting my fingers. I burned my dinner and my mouth as well.

The next day, as the weight of the pack took its toll, my emotions surfaced. I was angered by the weight of the pack—but I had packed it. My finger ached and my mouth hurt—but it was I who was to blame. I was becoming totally frustrated, but there was no one onto whom I could shift the blame. I yelled loudly and cursed a rock that tripped me. A branch that whipped my arm I punished by breaking it. Feelings and emotions started to flow freely, and they were all mine, without any distortion except what came from my mind. Nature was only reflecting what I took to it.

The next afternoon, as I watched storm clouds begin to form overhead, I decided that even if it did rain I would walk through it. But with the rain came a fifteen-degree drop in temperature. Bolts of lightning seared the sky. I was above the tree line and completely exposed to the elements, a victim of my own arrogance and ignorance. And I was scared. For the first time in my life, I was afraid of dying. The thunder, when it came, caused me to stumble by its sheer force. It took me three hours to reach a shelter, cold, tired, and scared. I had to take the next day off to dry everything out, and was only able to do this because some unknown hiker before me had had the foresight to leave firewood in a dry, secure spot under the shelter.

From this experience I learned to respect nature. In so doing I had to learn something about nature. The states of nature, whether raging or peaceful, are not good or bad but are expressions of magnificent power. In finding respect for nature I also found a new respect for myself. As I began to take responsibility for understanding the physical environment, it in turn gave me an understanding of my physical being, my body, and a unique glimpse of the power of mental forces over physical functioning. That glimpse allowed me to understand that we are indeed not our bodies, but neither are we solely our minds.

By the time I arrived in Hot Springs, North Carolina, I had blisters on all of my toes, two of which were infected, two strained knees, and abdominal pains. It took a few days and the help of a local doctor to recover sufficiently so that I could continue on. During the forced rest I reduced the weight in my pack to under forty-five pounds and made plans to upgrade my equipment at the first possible chance. I had begun to see my body as servant to my mind. My body would perform as best it could when asked, but it also had limitations and needs, which had to be heeded. Each morning that I drew on my boots over blistered and infected toes, the pain was excruciating, but I would not let my mind be ruled by the pain. I acknowledged it, then let it go. After a short time I did not notice the pain until the end of the day, at which point I would bathe my feet. Once I was able to see my body as a separate aspect, a servant, I also understood that I was responsible for the maintenance and upkeep of this machine. To this day I keep my body supplied with all that it needs.

Once I had shed the extra pack weight and informed my body of what I needed it to do, I was able to establish a rhythm, one that was in line with the rhythm of nature.

Everything had a flow, no problem was insurmountable. Often things fell into place as if by magic. Whatever I needed—a good resting place on the trail, shelter, companionship, or the cessation of an emotional state—would appear just when I needed it. This happened so frequently that I began to call it "trail magic."

My emotions also were affected. In the early days I would swing from one extreme to another, from frustration to exuberance. After weeks of walking with myself as chief companion, however, I was able to watch the play of my emotions in a more detached frame of mind. I became an observer of what seemed to be a separate mind as it carried on with its tantrums. I was no longer so affected emotionally as to react blindly, but instead I witnessed the "mind play" and then took the most logical course of action.

Humans are part of nature, and by being alone in nature we re-establish our connections with the natural flow. This flow has been disrupted by the life-styles we have become accustomed to in the modern age. Many of us have experienced the feeling of connectedness with nature as we enjoyed a pleasant, sunny day, but how many have felt that same connectedness while standing outside during a raging storm? Just as nature has natural swings in weather patterns, so humans experience natural swings in the emotions from our minds. But if we are out of rhythm with ourselves and nature we will become trapped by our own feelings and emotions. We will be lost.

On October 11th I stood on top of Mount Katahdin, in Maine. I had completed my physical journey. I had survived the usual discomforts, enjoyed "trail magic," and learned something about myself and my relation to the physical universe. But some of the most important lessons garnered from this experience are still taking shape years after the fact.

An important discovery I made on the trail was that we are not solely our bodies, nor are we solely our minds. Rather, body and mind are parts of what we are, parts that must serve a purpose. These tools must be studied and mastered if they are to be used efficiently. The purpose to which these tools are put is self-knowledge.

In *Tertium Organum,* the Russian philosopher P. D. Ouspensky stated that the meaning of life consists of knowledge: "All the mental faculties of man, all the elements of his inner life—sensations, representations, concepts, ideas, judgments, conclusions, feelings, emotions, even creation—all these are the instruments of the knowledge which we possess." Almost all religions and spiritual writings stress the importance of self-knowledge. Jesus said, "The kingdom of God is within you." The yogis of India say, "God dwells in you." If these statements are true, as I believe they are, then learning about yourself will lead you to God or, if you prefer, truth—the truth of your own being.

I started on the path to self-knowledge by accepting responsibility for my own life. I started with something concrete, something I knew about—my body. Caring for my body included getting enough exercise and rest, and choosing a better diet. The simple needs of the body, often overlooked in the grand scheme of things, led me to consider the mind and its needs. The food I consume affects my mind, and so does the information I allow myself to take in. By learning about myself on the physical level, I have also supplied my mind with healthy information. Similarly, as I learned more about the workings of the human mind, it opened the door to something else—the spiritual aspect of man. So, anything I learn affects more than one level.

One of the hardest experiences during this period of my life was awakening to the fact that society does not acknowledge the individual's need to understand the self, nor does it allow the individual proper time to undertake this task. Ideally it should be built into the social structure, so that as one develops in society one also develops individually. That is rarely possible. Societal pressures generally force us either to accept society as it is or to become an outcast. And although I have constructed my life in such a way that I am able to continue on the path that I have chosen, the external pressure still makes itself known. I know in my heart that my path is right, but it takes commitment and persistence to follow this path when all the while society refuses to accept it or me.

The Way of the Tarot

Walking the Appalachian Trail had given me an abundance of new insights into myself. The following summer I decided to look for a place where I could take some time to think about my experience without distraction. I found that place in upstate New York at Omega, an institute for holistic studies. It was described in the catalogue as a place for healing and self-transformation. The rest of the description seemed equally promising. At Omega, people from all over the world came together to dispense knowledge on topics from sports to spirituality. In such a setting, I thought, I might find other people who could help me in my search for knowledge. I applied for a summer staff job at Omega, and was hired.

Never before had I experienced anything quite like this place. I went there intending to reflect on my experiences in the woods, but the opportunities for learning in the various workshops helped redirect and focus my search in new ways. It was at Omega, while taking a workshop, that I was introduced to Christian Hermeticism, a school of thought that deals with philosophical, theological, and occult subjects. The origins of the Hermetic tradition have been traced back to somewhere between 50 and 300 A.D. The school of thought is based on the writings of a much older, pre-Christian figure, Hermes Trismegistus, thought to be equivalent to Thoth, the Egyptian god of wisdom.

It was the description in the catalogue that drew me to this workshop. It mentioned that the human will and imagination could be developed and used for spiritual growth. I saw this as an opportunity to further my understanding of the will and imagination.

The book used in the course was called *Meditations on the Tarot*. Written by an anonymous author and published posthumously, *Meditations on the Tarot* explores the tarot deck as a source of wisdom and knowledge that has been passed down through time via the cards. The book refers to the images on the cards as authentic symbols that, when meditated on, activate the inner depths of the soul. Through these ancient symbols one can come to experience and understand the mysteries of the self.

Symbols have proved a potent mechanism for twentieth-century investigations into the mind. Perhaps the most famous user of symbols was Carl G. Jung. In Jungian thought, symbols are mediums that allow the expression of thoughts that cannot be expressed in words. Symbols promote understanding by mediating between the known and the unknown.

The tarot deck is the forerunner of the present-day deck of playing cards. It has four suits, coins, cups, wands, and swords, which in the modern deck have become clubs, diamonds, spades, and hearts. Each suit also has a jack, queen, and king. These cards compose the minor arcana and also make up the conventional modern deck of fifty-two playing cards.

In addition to the minor arcana, the tarot deck has twenty-two pictorial cards that are referred to as the major arcana. It is the major arcana that *Meditations on the Tarot* uses in its inquiry.

The singular form of arcana, arcanum, is defined by Webster's as "mysterious knowledge known only to the initiate." The word is related to arcane and also to ark, a vessel which holds mysterious or sacred knowledge. *Meditations on the Tarot* defines an arcanum as "that which it is necessary to 'know' in order to be fruitful in a given domain of spiritual life."

Meditations on the Tarot discusses the way of knowledge of each of the major arcana and uses the arcana to stir the individual's imagination toward spiritual growth. The anonymous author saw each card as a separate spiritual exercise that, when used as an object for meditation, would open doors into one's own spiritual life. Taken together, the cards represent a school in the "art of learning" through the process of meditation.

Although a deck of tarot cards did not at first seem to me to be a viable way of learning about my experience, the method nevertheless dealt with other issues I was very much interested in, such as the roles of imagination, concentration, and will. Not until much later, when I started to learn about the function of myths in human life, did I become aware of the immense potential of the cards as a learning tool. Meditating on the tarot cards broadened my perspective. Instead of being limited to my singular existence, which covered only about thirty-five years and was bounded by societal norms, I was able to project my experiences into the totality of human spiritual experience throughout time. This long historical view, which I could not have developed on my own, helped me make sense of my individual life.

◉

On the first day of class we were told to choose a card from the tarot deck without looking. The card I picked was the Magician, the first card in the deck. I had to smile as the memory of being a "wizard's wizard" came to mind. At least I was being consistent!

By virtue of its position as the first card in the deck, the Magician is key to understanding the rest of the cards. The author described the Magician card as follows:

> The first Arcanum—the principle underlying all the other twenty-one Major Arcana of the Tarot—is that of the rapport of personal effort and of spiritual reality. It occupies the first

place in the series because if one does not understand it (i.e., take hold of it in cognitive and actual practice), one would not know what to do with all the other Arcana. For it is the Magician who is called to reveal the practical method relating to all the Arcana.

In other words, meditating on the Magician helps the individual become aware of the attitudes and the state of mind that are necessary to begin an in-depth study of the tarot.

As I continued to read and understand the implications of studying the tarot, I began to notice similarities between my experience when projected into the cards and the interpretation of various cards by the book's author. For example, the author suggests that the Magician card gives us a way to grasp "the reality of the spirit." This process of understanding is summed up in the formula,

Learn first concentration without effort, transform work into play, make every yoke that you have accepted easy and every burden that you carry light.

In Chapter 7 I discussed the importance of concentration in Theron Dumont's conception of the spiritual experience and in my own experience. Concentration has also been accorded importance by modern psychotherapy and in various spiritual practices throughout the world. By learning how to concentrate, we as individuals can begin to control the free thoughts and spontaneity of our imagination. It is the inability to control the thought and imagination during a manic episode that results in the individual's inability to stay within his normal reality.

Meditations on the Tarot also tells us that "will . . . is the determining and decisive factor in concentration." The author describes "concentration without effort" as a shift of awareness on the part of the individual from the thinking center of his mind to the feeling center of his heart: "It is the profound silence of desires, of preoccupation, of the imagination, of the memory and of discursive thought."

I understand this idea as meditation in motion. When I take time out of my day to sit down and meditate, the state I experience seems to be the same state as mentioned here. In other words, "concentration without effort" suggests a constant state of meditation even as one is functioning in the physical world. The innermost being remains focused while the physical being goes on with its worldly tasks. In this fashion, work becomes play. When the individual aligns himself with his spiritual aspect, he creates a "zone of silence" in which he is connected to a higher source. This connection allows him to accept and execute any responsibility that comes his way.

The Magician card, because it represents a synthesis of the conscious and the unconscious, acts as a bridge between these two worlds. In learning about human spirituality, we inevitably find ourselves caught between the known world and the unknown world. Once we have succeeded in putting this bridge into place, once we have merged the ego self with the unconscious self, we have achieved what Jungian psychologists call "individuation."

How exactly are we to erect this bridge between the conscious and the unconscious, between the known world and the unknown world? What techniques are available to us in this task? To answer this question we must back up a little.

I have mentioned that according to the Russian philosopher P. D. Ouspensky, the meaning of life consists in knowledge.

Meditations on the Tarot suggests that the aim of all knowledge is the truth, and that the truth relies on

> the reduction of the plurality of phenomena to an essential unity—of facts to laws, of laws to principles, of principles to essence or being. All search for truth—mystical, gnostic, philosophical and scientific—postulates its existence, i.e., the fundamental unity of the multiplicity of phenomena in the world.

The fundamental unity of all things is illuminated through analogy. Analogy uncovers relationships, sometimes hidden ones, between things. Analogy thus becomes the ideal tool for moving into the unknown and assimilating it to our experience of the known.

Meditations on the Tarot describes analogy this way:

> Analogy is not a tenet or postulate—the essential unity of the world is this—but is the first and principal method (the aleph of the alphabet of methods) whose use facilitates the advance of knowledge.

One of the greatest contributions of the tarot may be this understanding of analogy as a way to blaze new trails of knowledge. By using the symbols on the tarot cards, I was able to project my experiences of mania through the cards in such a way that my experiences became available for intellectual understanding.

◎

Meditations on the Tarot describes four distinct stages of investigation of truth, the mystical, gnostic, magical, and philosophical stages. In my third experience of mania I found myself caught in three worlds, which I defined at the time as mystical, magical, and linear. As it turned out, this was more than just coincidence. I was finding connections through this path that started to pull everything together for me. My experiences began to follow a structured course.

Meditations on the Tarot states that the pure mystical experience cannot be directly understood, that it must be filtered through the process of reflection (meditation) which renders it understandable to consciousness. The pure mystical experience comes about when the individual "dares to aspire to the supreme reality." In my case, this happened when I decided I wanted to be god. Mania, at least in part, constitutes a pure mystical experience in which the known meets the unknown. It presents to the individual another reality, one that cannot be immediately understood. The process of reflection makes the pure, unmediated mystical experience available to the conscious mind, to the intellect. The transformation of the mystical experience into an assimilable experience is subsumed under the term "gnosis." Gnosis means "knowledge," and it is in the gnostic stage that an individual is able to perceive the mystical experience as a "message" or "inner word." In my experience, the gnostic stage was skipped. I did not have the presence of mind to reflect on my experience.

After the gnostic stage, during which the individual formulates an understanding of his experience, he may chose to put this understanding into practice. If he does so, he steps into the magical stage.

The magical stage is followed by the philosophical stage. In this stage the mystical experience, having become accessible to the conscious mind through gnosis and put into practice in the magical stage, undergoes yet another transformation, this one of form: it becomes a communicable symbol. Communication may take the form of teaching or writing. As it is communicated, the mystical experience is also formulated, not in the sense of a cut-and-dried directive but in the sense of something that has been expressed and so made available to the community outside of the person who has had the experience.

These four stages, the mystical, gnostic, magical, and philosophical, constitute a structure of knowledge. The stages are linked together by analogy, which helps the individual move from one stage to the next. Although my understanding of this structure of knowledge comes from studying the tarot, I believe it is generally applicable to the way humans learn about themselves and their world.

Once the individual who has experienced the mystical, mania, has been able to understand the essence of this experience, he has taken a step toward becoming an authority of the experience. According to *Meditations on the Tarot,* "Authority . . . is the magic based on gnosis due to mystical experience." Who other than the one who has had a mystical experience can render knowledge and understanding of that experience? The process of gnosis, if one chooses the responsibility, may take years of constant thought and searching before any understanding is available, and there is always the possibility that the experience may never be completely understood.

As I continued working with the tarot, my attention was drawn to other areas of interest, such as the will. *Meditations on the Tarot* suggests that the individual, by using his or her will, can create within him- or herself a space for "illumination" to be received as the personal will comes into line with the universal will. To create such a space, the individual would have to establish an attitude of service. In so doing, we as individuals can enter into a working union with nature, becoming part of it instead of trying to control it. This working union in turn acts as a guiding force. The idea of service is a cardinal principle of the religious orders that tend to serve people. The act of service in turn creates humility, which has always been a part of, and prerequisite to, any spiritual path.

By aligning oneself with the "creative principle" of nature, one can begin to heal the split that science has created by trying to control nature. In healing this split, we open ourselves to receive from nature the gifts that nature has always offered. I experienced this in part during my time in the woods. As I adjusted my physical, mental, and spiritual aspects to be in line with the rhythm of nature, I learned a different way of being, not only with myself but with the world in general. I called it "trail magic," because it was so astonishing to me, but now I see it as the natural state of things. It is not magic but life.

The mystical experience cannot be entered into by any means other than grace from above. *Meditations on the Tarot* states, "There is no faith, hope, and love without mystical experience or, what is the same thing, without grace." But preparedness for grace or for "initiation" is important. Preparedness marks the difference between the mystical experience that is properly understood and the mystical experience that is entered into without training or understanding, such as during mania.

The mystical experience—in my case, mania—can now be understood as aligned with grace, grace being defined as a gift from above. From the mystical experience comes faith, which in turn provides hope for that part of man that lies seemingly beyond our reach, hope for a love in the union of man and God.

Each of the tarot cards allowed me to associate certain characteristics of mania with the spiritual path as pictured in the cards. For the first time, I could begin to interpret certain images, feelings, and thoughts that came to me during mania in a system that lent itself to this purpose. I was able to view mania as an initiation, an act of grace from above, instead of as an illness. This view released me from the limiting ideas and structure that had been imposed on me by the hospitals that treated me. I was freed to follow a line of thought that had no limiting prejudices other than the ones I brought to it myself.

Throughout *Meditations on the Tarot,* the text draws parallels between the spiritual significance of the cards and the research of Carl Jung. Through this connection, I was able to move from an "ethereal" stage of thought down to a "corporeal" stage of thought. In the following chapter I discuss the work of Carl Jung as it relates both to the spiritual aspect of man and to my experiences.

The anonymous author of *Meditations on the Tarot* mentioned mania specifically. In the author's terminology, mania consists of inflation, a superiority complex, and megalomania. In relation to my work and experience, these terms correlate with the hypomanic, manic, and psychotic phases of mania. These are all "trials" that the individual must undergo while traveling the spiritual path.

The mystical experience expresses itself in three different forms. The first is the union with nature, where the individual begins to feel him- or herself as a piece of the external world. The second form is the union with the transcendental Self, where the individual's higher self is experienced as immortal and free. The last form is a union with God, which is experienced through the oneness of love.

In attaining these three unities, the individual will be aided by humility. Humility keeps in check the tendency to be carried away by inflation. The spiritual and religious orders of today are aware of the importance of humility and develop this virtue in their charges, primarily through the course of selfless service. Humility, in the terms of the tarot, "implies consciousness of the difference and distance between the center of human consciousness and the center of divine consciousness."

The course I took at Omega and the book, *Meditations on the Tarot,* gave me a concrete, organized system that allowed me to see my experience of mania from a different perspective other than illness. It validated my constant efforts of the previous years, during which I felt completely alone and misunderstood. It gave me the support and energy that I needed to continue my personal search. By guiding me to Carl Jung's work, it helped me relate my esoteric thoughts to accepted avenues of study in psychology. I began to see that my views on my experiences, which ran contrary to everyone else's views, were without a doubt absolutely true. This conviction is still with me today, although I cannot rightly express it in words. And even today, as I continue my search, a mixture of emotions—rage, frustration, love, self-respect—still finds its way into my consciousness. But I have come to accept these feelings for what they are and have come a long way toward understanding who I am.

Jung's Structure of the Psyche

As Christian Hermeticism, which I learned of through studying *Meditations on the Tarot,* "steps down" into modern psychology, it makes the age-old teachings of the Gnostics and spiritualists available for modern humans to use in their personal development. The other side of the coin, of course, is modern psychology "stepping up" into spiritualism by taking note of the needs of the spirit as an essential part of human growth.

Carl G. Jung provided the important link that would "step up" modern psychology into spirituality. Jung, who died in 1961, was a colleague of Sigmund Freud. He worked with Freud for eight years, until insurmountable differences over religion and the role of sexuality in human life led to a severing of the relationship. Jung's important contribution to analytical psychology was to introduce the idea of man's spiritual existence into the mainstream of psychological thought.

Jung is perhaps best known for his use of myths and dream symbols as larger structures for addressing the psychic integrity—the "wholeness"—of an individual person. Some of the terms he coined or gave new life to, such as collective unconscious and archetype, have entered the common vocabulary of people the world over. His daring insistence on spirituality continues to fill a void in modern analytic practice.

After reading *Meditations on the Tarot,* I was ready for a modern application, some contemporary thought that would speak directly to the condition of modern man striving for spirituality, for the conditions of life today seem set against the practice and experience of spirituality. I was interested to find a link to the tarot in Jung, for Jung understood the pictorial symbols of the tarot as descendants of ancient "archetypes of transformation." In *The Archetypes*

115

and the Collective Unconscious, Jung described archetypes of transformation as "not personalities, but . . . typical situations, places, ways and means, that symbolize the kind of transformation in question." In this chapter I discuss some of the processes involved in Jungian psychic transformation and relate them to my understanding of what occurs during mania.

INDIVIDUALIZATION AND TRANSFORMATION

Jung described psychological growth as a "process of individualization" whereby the totality of the individual is realized. Individualization is achieved by the conscious and the unconscious working together in constant expression, neither one dominating the other. This process, once it is in place, re-centers the being from the ego to what Jung referred to as the "Self."

In *Introduction to a Science of Mythology,* Jung addressed the relationship between the ego and the Self that reflects the totality of the individual:

> The "superordinate personality" is the total man, i.e., man as he really is, not as he appears to himself. To this wholeness the unconscious psyche also belongs, which has its requirements and needs just as the consciousness has. . . . I usually describe the "superordinate personality" as the "self," thus making a sharp distinction between the ego, which, as is well known, extends only as far as the conscious mind, and the whole of the personality, which includes the unconsciousness as well as the conscious component. The ego is thus related to the "self" as a part to the whole. To that extent the self is superordinate.

116

Moreover, the self is felt empirically not as subject but as object, and this by reason of its unconscious component, which can only come to consciousness indirectly, by way of projection.

In this passage Jung clearly distinguished between the "Self," which includes both the conscious and the unconscious aspects of the mind, and the ego, which is only the conscious part of the mind.

As I have related earlier, in all three of my manic experiences I had the sensation of sitting back and watching my mind function on a higher level than it had ever functioned before. It was as if I had two minds. I became both the observer and the observed. When I did not make the adjustment—when I did not, in Jung's terminology, re-center from the ego to the Self—the result was a form of inflation. This inflation has also been called—by the anonymous author of *Meditations on the Tarot*—"identifying with the hero."

Jung understood that inflation is one of the perils that an individual faces in the process of individualization. Inflation, if not checked, can swell to become megalomania. In the state of inflation, the individual identifies the Self with the ego.

Inflation seems to be characteristic of the hypomanic phase of mania. In my case, as my mind "opened," my sense of self-importance also ballooned, leading me to wonder if I was a genius, and ultimately directing me to believe that I was God, or godlike. The "opening" that I experienced was my awareness of a higher self, and my identification of my ego with this higher self was the confusion that led me into mania. *Meditations on the Tarot* describes the confusion of the selves, and the consequent megalomania, this way:

117

The "higher Self" is then experienced as the supreme and unique Self of the world, although it is only higher in relationship to the ordinary, empirical self, and it is far from the supreme and unique being . . . far from being God, in other words.

Aggrandizement of the Self, and a superiority complex that leads to megalomania, seem to be frequent accompaniments of an "awakening." They appear to be necessary trials that the individual must pass through en route to giving birth to the new Self.

In the early years of my search, and especially during episodes of mania, I did not know how to separate my ego from the Self, or even that such a separation was necessary. Furthermore, the transition from the ego to the Self appears to the ego as its death. So, unless the individual is first capable of understanding the process of individualization and then develops a fully mature ego structure, he or she cannot possibly make a smooth transition.

Jung made a pivotal point when he alluded to the fact that human consciousness grows out of the unconscious. Our physiology is geared to such a transfer: In humans, the sleep-wake cycle allows the unconscious to influence the consciousness through dreams. Jung believed that psychological growth depends largely on the ability of the individual to make available to the conscious mind the content of the unconscious mind.

The Jungian process of re-centering, then, requires that the individual be able to make the transition from the unconscious to the conscious continuously and with ease. The fluid passage from the unconscious to the conscious, with each aspect wide awake to the other, is the culmination of the process of individualization. It is also what Thomas Hudson referred to as the state of genius.

How does one make this transition? One answer is found in both *Meditations on the Tarot* and Rudolf Steiner's *Knowledge of the Higher Worlds:* through work and worship. I gained some insight into the formidable balancing powers of "work and worship" during my second episode, when I did not progress from hypomania to mania. The work I had set for myself became my total focus and meditation, in which the quotidian is relinquished in favor of a state "above" the usual distractions, can be considered a form of prayer.

Involvement in work creates a structure in which the energy that is produced during mania is channeled. Since work is physical and tangible, it will prevent the individual from being carried away by inflation, for the results are readily seen. The expression of the unconscious can only be measured by the results the individual produces in his or her work. The anonymous author of *Meditations on the Tarot* depicts this best:

> Worship and work constitute the only curative as well as pro-phylactic remedy that I know against megalomania illusions. It is necessary to worship what is above us and it is necessary to participate in human effort in the domain of objective facts in order to be able to hold in check the illusions concerning what one is and what one is capable of. For whoever is aware of raising his prayer and meditation to the level of pure wor-ship will always be conscious of the distance which separates (and at the same time unites) the worshipper and the wor-shipped. Therefore he will not be tempted to worship himself, which is in the last analysis the cause of megalomania. He will

always have in sight the distance between himself and the worshipped. He will not confuse what he is with what the worshipped being is.

On the other hand, he who works, i.e., who takes part in human effort, with a view to objective and verifiable results, will not fall prey to illusion with respect to what he is capable of.

Thus, during the course of achieving individualization, the continuous flow between the unconscious and the conscious must have a regulator that will transform the tremendous power of the unconscious into a viable source of energy. That regulator is "work and worship."

THE COLLECTIVE UNCONSCIOUS

One of Jung's major contributions to modern psychology was the recognition of the collective unconscious. The collective unconscious, according to Jung, is inherited and not the possession of any individual; it is universal. It stands in sharp contrast to the personal unconscious, which is a superficial layer of consciousness that emerges from the personal experiences of the individual. The collective unconscious affords a second psychic structure that is based on modes of behavior that are the same for all men.

Jung used the term archetypes to identify the forms that exist in the collective unconscious. These forms are always present and have an indirect influence on all individuals. Jung's idea of the collective unconscious is supported by the appearance of the same behavioral motifs in myths and fairy tales of human cultures. Even myths arising in different cultures and in different eras seem to express the same universal themes.

In *The Archetypes and the Collective Unconscious,* Jung defined an archetype as follows:

> The archetype is essentially an unconscious content that is altered by becoming conscious and by being perceived, and it takes its colour from the individual consciousness in which it happens to appear.

This concept of an archetype as a separate but real psychic structure has relevance when applied to my third episode, when I experienced myself as a "wizard." I now believe my identification with a wizard was the expression of psychic material whose source was the collective unconscious (as manifested in my mind), and that the particular archetype being figured was the Magician. In *Introduction to a Science of Mythology,* Jung wrote,

> The archetype—let us never forget this—is a psychic organ present in all of us. A bad explanation means a correspondingly bad attitude to this organ, which may thus be injured. The ultimate sufferer is the bad interpreter himself. Hence the "explanation" should always be such that the functional significance of the archetype remains unimpaired, i.e., that an adequate and appropriate relationship between the conscious mind and the archetypes is ensured.

Because I did not know how to acknowledge the archetype as an archetype, which would have allowed me to understand it as a symbol, I identified with the archetype.

This identification disrupted my psychological balance. It prompted me to believe I was a hero figure, which in turn led to a second identification. In Jung's words,

> The epiphany of the hero (second identification) shows itself in a corresponding inflation: the colossal pretension grows into a conviction that one is something extraordinary, or else the impossibility of the pretension ever being fulfilled only proves one's own inferiority, which is favorable to the role of the heroic sufferer (a negative inflation). In spite of their contrariety, both forms are identical, because unconscious compensatory inferiority tallies with conscious megalomania, and unconscious megalomania tallies with conscious inferiority (you never get one without the other).

If the first identification is not avoided, inflation (or hypomania) is experienced. This inflation, if it is not curtailed, then leads to the second identification (or mania). A potential third step in this progression is becoming psychotic.

Positive inflation and negative inflation, in my experience, are tied in to manic-depression. One of the things I did not understand at the time was that negative inflation should be present. Even if it is unconscious, it should have some form of expression. But I had had only manic experiences. This bothered me for a time until I discovered that negative inflation was in fact present and expressing itself through various unconscious avenues. By my inability to grieve or accept my brother's death, I was keeping myself from being overwhelmed, thus preventing severe depression.

THE VOICE OF THE UNCONSCIOUS

Jung suggested that the unconscious speaks to us through symbols. The speech commonly occurs in dreams, and the symbols carrying the message emerge from dream imagery. A symbol suggests something more than what is immediately apparent. In Chapter 9 I discussed the tarot cards as symbols that, when meditated on, allow the individual to access his or her unconscious. By using the tarot this way, I was able to understand certain confusing aspects of mania.

By using the language of the unconscious, or symbols, we can stimulate this part of our psyche to enter into an active dialogue with the conscious. The difficulty that arises in this form of dialogue is that the individual's ability to interpret the symbolic messages from the unconscious may be insufficiently developed. Because the dream symbols are different for everyone, the individual must make a constant and thorough inquiry into his or her own dreams. This is a considerable task, and one that is daunting to begin.

The spiritual aspect of human consciousness described by Jung can be related to *Meditations on the Tarot,* where this spiritual aspect is noted in its mystical, gnostic, and magical components. Jung's process of individualization is the same process that is involved when one aspires to become a Magician (or any other figure in the major arcana) and in so doing begins a journey into the unconscious. Jung also noted that the spiritual aspect of man can cause various psychic disorders. My experiences with mania, when viewed from either the Jungian standpoint or the structure of psychic growth outlined in *Meditations on the Tarot,* become understandable.

In connection with the use of archetypes as tools for developing psychically, I would like to mention an incident that occurred during my second experience. During this time I wrote several letters home. In one correspondence I wrote,

> It seems that I have a highly sensitive part of my brain that, for now, I'll call THOTH, so that I can refer to it readily as a separate entity. Now THOTH seems to be very sensitive . . . but at the same time he is extremely intelligent. . . .

Jung specifically mentioned Thoth as an archetypal figure, referring to him as a "wise old man." You will remember that in my second episode I did not go psychotic. I did not become Thoth—I understood him as a separate entity. In other words, I maintained a distance between myself and the archetype. In my third episode, by contrast, I became a "wizard's wizard," identifying with an archetypal figure. This identification disrupted my psychological balance and, I believe, contributed to my manic state.

My discovery of Jung, coming hard on the heels of my learning about the tarot symbols, helped me place my personal experiences within the totality of human experience. Understanding that I was part of a larger reality caused a paradigm shift in the way I thought about myself and the world. No longer were my experiences unique aberrations that placed me at the edge of humanity. Instead, these experiences became folded into the process of psychic growth that is available to anyone and that many people before me, in every age, have experienced.

Final Episode

During that summer at Omega I had the opportunity to meet several spiritual leaders and hear them speak. Whether Buddhist, Zen, Sufi, or of some other calling, all seemed to carry the same truth, but in different interpretations. At Omega I also experienced the sense of work as play. Work was no longer a burden or something to be avoided but a joy to participate in because it connected me with the Omega community. Being at Omega gave me invaluable opportunities to learn, and the only cost was to exchange work for my stay. So in the summer of 1989 I again worked at Omega, and in this summer I had my last uncontrolled episode of mania.

This experience did not follow the same pattern as the previous three experiences. Over the course of the summer I had been receiving body work at least once a week and was involved in other activities that allowed emotional release. There was no single experience I can point to as the trigger for this episode. It appeared to come on gradually over a period of nine weeks. Looking back, I can see certain unrelated incidents that pointed to the onset of another episode, such as the small emotional releases that I experienced during group sessions and the lack of physical exercise. I was eating a vegetarian diet and meditating consistently during this period, so the controls of diet and mental rest were in place. I also became involved in yoga. At the time I did not know that yoga is also release work for the body and emotions.

The fourth episode started on July 22. I was riding in a car when I felt my mind begin to swell, just as it had in my previous experiences. I became very nervous and wanted to return to campus to take a nap. When I got back to campus I started to experience a release of emotions that just seemed to overflow from my consciousness. This phase lasted forty-five minutes to an hour. I was with a group of friends who watched over me and made sure that I ate and rested.

Over the next few days my enthusiasm and energy level increased. I did not have the feeling of being a genius, but my heart chakra, or heart center, was completely open. I find this experience particularly hard to explain. I had the sensation that we were all one and I could "see" the want in everyone to express this oneness, but at the same time I "saw" the fear that blocked expression, a fear that could only be overcome by having the courage to express love. The desire to be one was universal, but so was the fear. The children at the institute had less fear, or rather seemed more open to accepting love, than the adults. Adults needed a little more time to make the decision to open up. This feeling stayed with me for a few days. At times I felt so much love that I became "blissed out." I can find no other term to describe the incredible feeling in my heart.

After this period came an opposite swing in my emotions. I became quite upset with my co-workers, almost to the point of rage. This behavior made me feel both guilty and ashamed, but I did not seem to have any control over my emotions. They just poured out on their own. Several people noticed my unusual behavior, confronted me with it, and told me to stay away from other people's energies and center myself.

I decided to drive home with a friend the following morning. On the way home my objective control started to slip. In the middle of the highway, for no reason I know of, I slammed on the brakes, bringing the vehicle to a complete stop. My friend decided I should not drive anymore and took over that responsibility.

My family had been notified by Omega that I had been acting strangely and was on my way home. I stayed home for two days before my actions got so out of hand that my family was compelled to call the hospital. During those two days at home I was seeing God in everyone. Whoever appeared to be in control I addressed as God. The appellation jumped from person to person, depending on the authority each one seemed to have. I also noticed something else, something I could not mention because I did not know how to express it. I was conscious of a total balance in each moment, no matter what was going on. Everything was in harmony with everything else.

The hospital sent a crisis team to the house, and the decision was made to put me in the hospital. I was put in a room with several other people. My mind was racing with paranoia and fear. I had a hard time staying focused on any one thing or person. I finally centered myself and asked to speak to the person in charge. I told her I was scared, and asked her please to tell me what was going to happen. She reassured me that everything was fine and that I would be okay. I told her I needed to know what would be done because I felt that I was going to lose control. As I forced myself to focus on her, I was able to contain my paranoia. She told me that one nurse would administer a shot to each of my arms. I believed her. As I waited for this to happen the same woman, who was in charge, decided that the nurse was taking too long and proceeded to administer one of the shots herself. She had lied to me! I almost became violent; then I just gave up. As I waited to be wheeled away, I looked at this woman and repeated a childhood rhyme: "Liar, liar, your tongue will split, and all the little doggies will have a little bit." It was my only way to respond to what I felt was a poor handling of the situation by the head of the department.

Two weeks later the hospital released me. I was back on lithium. I did not know what to do. It would take a little more time after this experience before I could gather up the courage to continue my search. I did not know what had triggered the episode. It seemed to have built up over time, perhaps over the entire eighteen months since my last episode. Perhaps I was wrong, and mania was an illness after all. This question continues to haunt me. I am the only person I know who continues to deny that mania is an illness, but I must always keep in mind that further information might prove me wrong. Certainly through my fourth experience, everything seemed to indicate that mania was an illness.

"Yes, you can. You can do this." The memory of those words, which I had heard during my third episode, would not let me give up. They comforted me in my solitude and strengthened me in my belief. Again I was confronted with a dilemma. If I really believed in what I was trying to prove, then taking lithium could only be detrimental, both physically and psychologically. Although the decision this time took a little longer to make, I again stopped taking lithium. As before, nothing happened to my mind. Everything stayed the same.

Personal Work

Shortly after my fourth episode, a friend asked me if I had done any personal work. I did not understand what he was asking. I believed that researching my manic experiences was personal work, but this was not what he was referring to.

The following year I came to the conclusion that I could not go on trying to solve my problems alone. I needed help. I had a hard time making the decision to seek help because in one way I regarded it as giving up. But I could no longer deny that there were emotional problems that seemed to have some connection with my mania. Even this thought seemed treacherous, seemed to acknowledge that mania was an illness. It meant "they" were right and I was wrong. But I drew some reassurance from the memory of a lecture I had attended at Omega by Ram Dass. Ram Dass, formerly a psychology professor at Harvard and a spiritual teacher, said that it did not matter how one got to another state of consciousness. It is the experience of the other state of consciousness that will direct one's subsequent search for self-understanding. How one comes by that experience has very little to do with it. It is the experience that is important.

One of my major concerns in finding help was that I hesitated to use the term "manic-depressive." I felt it automatically put me into a certain category, and once I was categorized I would not be treated as an individual. After attending many group meetings and listening to other people's stories, I felt that many cases labeled "manic-depressive" had nothing in common with my experiences. Manic-depression seemed to be a term used to cover a wide area of symptoms. In my opinion this was not only wrong but harmful as well.

My first step in beginning personal work was to move to a place where I could have space in which to work. I rented an apartment in a small town in New York State where I would have the time to put together a program to find out something about myself. My next task was to find a therapist. I did not know where to look for one, or even how. I did not have enough self-confidence to ask someone for a referral, so I just looked through the phone book and called a few places. I found someone close and started the ball rolling.

I did not know what to expect from therapy, but I did know that it would take time to develop a relationship with a therapist, so I agreed to two series of five sessions each. At the end of the second series I felt I was not getting anything accomplished. I felt as if I had wasted my time and a good deal of money besides. I was not sure if this was the result of my own unwillingness or of some lack in the therapist's capabilities. In any event, I looked around for someone else.

To the second therapist I revealed that I had been diagnosed as manic-depressive and was worried that my mania might be triggered by the therapy. I was told by the therapist that whatever needed to happen, would happen. This bland acceptance of possibly another round of mania and another hospitalization did not seem right or safe to me. It was in line with the approach of the people who ran the workshop on "Intuition and Psychic Development" in its irresponsibility. After three sessions I decided that the second therapist was not suitable for my needs either. I became so frustrated that I decided I could get better results on my own. I purchased a VCR and rented movies that would allow me to get in touch with some of my emotions. I experienced more pain and joy during this experiment than in all of my therapy combined, and at a fraction of the cost. I still needed a therapist, and knew I needed a therapist, but movies would have to do until I found one.

A KEY TURNS IN THE LOCK

While I was looking for a therapist I began to refocus attention on my diet. I had the feeling that something was missing. It had been close to ten years since I had begun restructuring my diet. I had removed all foods with chemical additives, carbonated beverages, red meat, and preservatives. But there were still things I did not understand. Why did I crave mushrooms in the winter but not in the summer? Why did I crave sweets at different times? Surely these things could be explained. There are reasons for everything, and someone had to know the reasons. So I began looking for someone who could explain to me how foods work.

Annemarie Colbin became that person. Colbin is the author of the book, *Food and Healing,* and the founder of the New York Natural Gourmet Cooking School. She is the only person I know who can answer not only these questions but many, many more. I was so impressed with her knowledge and her supportive health theory that I enrolled in her chef's training program to learn more about how foods not only affect the mind and body but also interact with other foods. And it was my interest in food and the cooking skills I learned from Annemarie Colbin that led me to my therapist. It came about the following way.

During the Christmas holidays that year I had the opportunity to stay at an ashram, a yoga retreat center, in the Bahamas. For ten days I was able to practice yoga and meditate in a community set up for that purpose. Although I had read about ashrams, this was my first experience visiting one. An ashram is the home of the spiritual leader of the sect that creates a space for individuals to develop along their spiritual paths through the practice of various yoga disciplines. There are four branches of yoga, any or all of which may aid the individual in spiritual growth. Karma yoga is the path of action. Bhakti yoga is the path of devotion. Jnana yoga is the use of the mind to inquire into its own nature, and Raja yoga is the science of mental and physical control. Ashrams encourage the practice of all four branches as a disciplined method of personal development. Although spiritual "awakenings" may sometimes occur with the practice of yoga, that is not the immediate goal.

I was interested in the workings of the ashram and decided to speak with one of the swamis, or spiritual teachers. Thinking of my own experience, I asked whether the ashram was prepared to handle someone who experienced a spiritual awakening. He answered yes, but I did not fully believe it. I came to the opinion that ashrams should be able to handle their followers if an awakening occurred because here, if anywhere, were people who should understand what was happening and know what to do. This would be the ideal function of an ashram. But unless there is a guru, or spiritual teacher, in residence who has experienced such an awakening, the ashram would not be able to serve this purpose.

The ashram offered programs for their guests every afternoon. The program one afternoon was called "Discovering the Inner Child." I attended this program to learn about this process, which I knew of only through my reading. A small group of about six people assembled for the workshop. I just wanted to observe, so I sat back and watched as the workshop progressed. I was amazed at the results, but more amazed by the technique the therapist, Natalie H. Rogers, used. She seemed able to take on the emotional response of the person with whom she was interacting and then mirror that response into her own feelings. If her response was the same as the other person's, the process would just unfold naturally. If her feeling was different, she would instruct that individual to express him- or herself in another form. An incident I witnessed will illustrate her method. One woman was experiencing a painful emotional issue and began crying, but the therapist did not mirror the same feeling of crying. Instead, she instructed the woman to verbalize her feelings rather than cry. Within a short time the woman was releasing an anger that was quite powerful, a completely opposite response to that of crying. I was very impressed with this therapist's method and asked if she would be interested in providing therapy sessions in exchange for my cooking. She agreed immediately, for she had been looking unsuccessfully for a vegetarian cook for some time. She, too, lived in New York, and we began working together the week after I returned home from vacation.

This therapist has been so providential that I still sometimes wonder why I went to cooking school in the first place. Was it so that I could find this therapist? Within weeks of our first session together she was able to point out different areas where I had blocked my own growth. I was incredibly relieved that at last somebody could see what I needed. I had been living on confusion and misunderstanding since childhood. The ways I had developed for coping with the world in childhood were still in place, but, as my therapist pointed out, they were no longer useful. They were hindering my growth. I had to replace these outdated defense mechanisms with new, mature ways of dealing with life. It was an incredible learning experience for me and one that led to a different perspective I had never realized existed.

My work with Natalie Rogers is described in Chapter 13, but I want to touch on some of the general aspects now. Under her guidance, I was able to stop being totally absorbed with myself and defending my every action. I learned to watch myself in different situations and then choose how I would respond. I started to gain control over my emotions not by denying them, as I had a tendency to do, but by expressing them in an appropriate manner that allowed me to release them and at the same time increase my self-respect. I was to learn that emotions and the mind are like everything else, tools that must first be understood and then mastered in order to be used properly. It was hard to let go of old immature patterns that in some cases still were effective. Those childhood defenses were comfortable. They were like old clothes: I could put them on without thinking. But their cost was high. In order to grow up I had to let the inappropriate childlike part of me die off. At times it seemed I would never untangle the ways of thinking I had created to survive, but overall I was able to adjust faster than I had anticipated. Once the problem is identified the correction does not take that long to put into place.

I worked with Natalie Rogers for three years. There were moments of failure but also moments of triumph in my personal growth work. At times I felt that I was on the cusp of a manic episode but was able to move away from it. I touched part of the grief over my brother's death, which had literally immobilized me. I was encouraged to go on working by the satisfaction that came with becoming a whole person again.

There are two ways to go out of your mind: through voluntary withdrawal, as in meditation, and through insanity. Many of the great spiritual masters of India were considered crazy at different times in their lives, not because they were able to withdraw from their minds, but because they were able to go out of their minds. I had the going-out-of-my-mind experience pushed on me involuntarily: I was pushed out of my head by the built-up forces of suppressed emotions. Now I had to learn what made me go out of my mind, or through my mind. I had to sort out the confusion and make the proper adjustments. Only in this way could I reach psychological maturity. But my confusion over what had happened to me did not take away from my experience of "awakening." Once initiation is given it remains, whether or not one chooses to follow that path. Everyone has a free will to choose.

COMING HOME

When I began therapy, I was still in cooking school. Occasionally I offered to drive home a fellow classmate of mine in cooking school. She was originally from France but was staying at an ashram in Manhattan. I was very interested in her experiences and asked her many questions about her life. During the course of one of these discussions she told me that she wanted to be God. I almost drove up on the sidewalk. I could not believe what I heard. She continued on, saying that we are all gods and that becoming God was essentially becoming who we really are. I didn't say anything, just listened to her. My mind was telling me, Look, she does not seem crazy, and you know that you are God, so what is the problem? I had a difficult time trying to find some stable ground to relate from.

My friend wanted to introduce me to her guru and continued to press this subject on subsequent rides home. I respectfully declined, not knowing exactly why but feeling that getting involved with a guru might not be a good idea. My friend mentioned that she would be spending the summer at an ashram in upstate New York that was associated with the one she was staying at in Manhattan. She would be working in the kitchen in the upstate ashram all summer. After much discussion I agreed to stop by the ashram when school was over.

I did not think any more about visiting the ashram and had not made plans to do so. Then one day in June when I had nothing else to do I thought of the ashram and called for information about their summer programs. I was informed that the spiritual leader, Gurumayi, would be speaking that night in her first program of the summer. I decided to attend the evening lecture.

The ashram was overflowing with people from all over the world. Hundreds of people had gathered together to hear Gurumayi speak. I found her to be a pleasant and gifted speaker. After her talk everyone lined up to receive her darshan, a blessing bestowed by a guru. As they approached her chair they knelt before her, touching their foreheads to the floor. I was amazed by this behavior. I had never before seen anything like it, and it was not to my liking. Although I did not get in line for a blessing, I did stay until everyone else had gone through the line, which seemed to go on for hours.

I continued to travel to the ashram each week to hear Gurumayi speak. I always found some truth to take home with me from her talks. It was openly taught at the ashram that we as individuals are gods, and that through the practice of yoga and the blessing of the guru, you would eventually attain your oneness.

After a couple of visits I decided to enroll in a three-day meditation course that combined talks by Gurumayi with periods of quiet meditation. On the first day I had a very moving experience. As I sat in meditation a feeling of satisfaction came over me. I felt very centered and at peace with myself. After a time a feeling of joy swept through my body, accompanied by the thought, I am coming home. I wept from relief, and from peace.

After the meditation was over, various people shared their life experiences with the group. During the discussion it emerged that a blue snake had been involved in several people's meditation. The mention of blue snakes raised a memory I had forgotten. Two years earlier a friend of mine had gone through a difficult period in her life, and at one point she told me she was seeing blue snakes that seemed to permeate her body. Neither she nor I knew anything about her experience. As the course at the ashram went on, I was to learn that seeing blue snakes is a common experience of people engaged in spiritual practices and should be viewed as a good sign in spiritual growth.

Along with the sitting meditation we also did chanting. Chanting is a spiritual exercise that increases the energy flow through the body. The chanting consisted of reciting a short verse, or mantra, over and over in a rhythmic flow. According to Baba Muktananda, Gurumayi's teacher, chanting purifies both the internal and the external atmospheres through the power of sound. Chanting has been studied in modern times, and it is said that certain sound vibrations do indeed have a positive effect on the health of the body.

After several minutes of chanting I could feel the energy flowing through me. It would rise and fall at different times during the exercise. After we finished chanting we sat quietly for another round of meditation. I had never before meditated with hundreds of people at the same time, and my meditation seemed to have a more powerful effect. These exercises produced in me a tremendous feeling of peace.

Although the spiritual practices of the ashram were new and somewhat strange to me, I had a favorable encounter with them, and I began reading the books written by Baba Muktananda. Muktananda took mahasamadhi, the Sanskrit word for death, in 1982, but before he died he wrote several books on the subject of spiritual paths. In *Play of Consciousness* he told the story of his life, framed in the progression through different levels of spiritual practices. He described the joyous times and the times of confusion, and gave a step-by-step account of his path. Over the next several months I learned a lot about the different aspects of spiritual practices from Muktananda's books.

◎

The period from September 1990 through August 1991 was a very powerful year for me in many ways. It was a year of consolidation, as well as a year of discoveries. It began with finding someone who could explain to me how food works. This information supplied me with the knowledge that had been missing in my investigation into the physical aspects of my life. Three months after finding someone who could tell me about food, I found my therapist. This therapist had both the knowledge and the desire to help me restructure my psyche and stop the vicious circle I was caught up in. Then, at the ashram, I learned an array of spiritual exercises that would allow me to set up a structure that I could follow.

Thus, the physical, mental, and spiritual branches of my search all came together over a period of one year. Ten years of constant searching and questioning came into focus in a logical way that I could understand and use. But as each piece of the puzzle fell into place, I still had to continue with the personal work, step by step. Much of that work still lay before me.

Warriors and Heroes

Finding a place to start in therapy can be confusing. Two people, two strangers, come together for one purpose. If the purpose is understood—and it is not always—the ways to this end are rarely clear. In my early work with Natalie H. Rogers I did not know what was expected of me. I approached therapy as I had approached everything else in the preceding ten years; by trying both to participate and to observe.

In my first few sessions with my therapist there was, to my mind, a power struggle. I would not now call it such, but at the time I thought of it this way. I would come in for my appointment, sit down, say nothing, and wait for my therapist to start. She, on the other hand, would sit across from me, expecting that I had come in with a situation to be worked out. It was a practical stalemate that led to my early refusal to trust her, and also highlighted my apparent need to be in control. I had a difficult time allowing somebody to help me. I felt that if I accepted help I would be "giving up," losing. My therapist tried to explain that my past experience was partly to blame for the way that I structured how I saw things. My reluctance to accept help, my fear of opening myself, was not wrong, it was what I did to protect myself from being hurt as a child. But that was then, and this was now. You are not a child anymore, she told me. You are an adult, and the systems that you set up to survive in childhood are not appropriate in the adult world. In fact, they are destructive ways of behaving.

Hearing this was one thing, understanding it as it related to my life was much harder. But over time I began to see very clearly that what she was saying was true. Eventually I was able to separate myself from my fears long enough to understand that certain things I had been doing and saying created, for better or worse, the reality in which I lived. This knowledge led to a tremendous feeling of freedom. Now I had to dismantle the immature, childish behavior and replace it with more appropriate, adult behavior. The results were astonishing. When I allowed myself to choose how I wanted to respond to a situation, to choose between the old way and some new way, I could feel the fear that always chose what worked in the past. But when I responded in a mature manner, not only did that fear not materialize, but I experienced a new sense of self-respect and empowerment. It was not always easy to let go of fears and known ways of doing things, but as time went on I learned to observe both ways of being.

One of the major goals in therapy, we both agreed, would be to keep me out of the hospital. To this end, during the first couple of months my therapist would not do any deep emotional work with me. Instead, we concentrated on physical controls. She noticed that when I became upset, I would begin to hyperventilate, breathing only with my chest. She sent me to a breath worker, with whom I worked for several weeks. I felt a little embarrassed going to someone to learn how to breathe, but in time I learned how to breathe correctly.

One of the areas I had to address early was allowing myself the right to state my feelings without having to defend them. I had to learn to say when something was bothering me instead of keeping it inside. At first I didn't understand what my therapist was trying to do. I had a tendency not to express the little things that annoyed me but to let them build up until I exploded. Forsaking this pattern was very hard for me. I tried to explain to my therapist that expressing trivial things was not what a man does. Instead, he makes an adjustment and deals with it, presumably by letting it go. Her view was just the opposite. When you state how you feel, she told me, no matter how trivial it may seem, you allow yourself to release it. If you do not acknowledge your feelings they get stuck. As they accumulate they become a powerful force that eventually must find an outlet, in my case by exploding. It was hard for me to incorporate this idea into my life because my resistance was so strong. Each time I wanted to verbalize my feelings I immediately condemned myself for being a baby, my feelings were not that big a deal.

Some of my difficulty in seeing and then changing this behavior pattern, I now believe, arose from my upbringing in a Catholic environment. I went to Mass on Sundays and attended Catholic schools from first grade through college. Guilt, shame, and the suppression of anger were part of the Catholic indoctrination. As I reviewed my growing up to see how different situations had been handled, I began to understand how and why I developed psychically as I did. My behavior was a defense against a Catholic-minded adult world that, with the best intentions, beat down children physically, mentally, and spiritually through its righteous, ignorant ways. As a child, I became a sneaky fighter. I would purposely become belligerent to authority, which was my only means of self-defense. If I could make the teachers or nuns become frustrated to the point of violence, I would see myself as a winner. And although I won more often than I lost, I always had to pay the price in their frustration and its consequences. Needless to say, I had a very hard time in school growing up. I was always at war.

Under the guidance of my therapist I began not only to try to express the trivial things before they built up, but also to experiment with forms of expression that were new to me. I joined public speaking forums and learned how to speak with authority and power in a way that was concise, thought out, and organized. I learned that the ability to formulate thoughts and express oneself verbally is a tremendous tool that can be used in all areas of life. I also tried out nonverbal forms of expression, such as drawing and painting. I enrolled in art classes, which taught me self-expression through a medium that was completely different from words, and which at times felt much more powerful and direct than words. Through these different paths of self-expression I also strengthened my concentration, which in turn facilitated the process of learning.

My therapist had noted my difficulty with adult figures as a child and now wanted to know who my heros were. What men did I look up to? What men gave me love or otherwise influenced my life in positive ways? I could not answer. Other than certain qualities that I admired in my father, I had no role model; there was no one person whom I wanted to be like. Most of my relationships with older men fell into the category of "I win, you lose." In light of what I was learning about my childhood defenses, I could understand why. I did not allow any other kind of relationship to materialize. Older men were authority figures, and I responded to authority by fighting it. I could count on the fingers of one hand older men whom I respected. I find it interesting to go back over my life and isolate the times when older men actually helped me. At the time, I did not understand why they were doing it. I knew only that it felt extremely good when the rare individual took an interest in me or asked my opinion on something. As I have matured, I have come to see these men as true men, reaching out from their hearts to help a child. The others—those who were not mature enough to see through a boy's fears—were immature boys themselves, incapable of giving something they themselves had never received.

Because there was no one in my personal life I could emulate, my next assignment was to go to the library and select bibliographies of great men to read. I picked an array of different men to study—Theodore Roosevelt, Winston Churchill, Malcom X, Kahlil Gibran, Vincent Van Gogh, Martin Luther King, Jr., Mikhail Gorbachev, Anwar Sadat. I learned who these men were, what shaped their lives, and how they learned and grew. These men in turn shaped the world we live in. I discovered that great men possess both good and bad characteristics and that there are many different but equally worthwhile ways of conducting one's life. My therapist told me to choose one of these men and let that person be my role model for a time. I chose Winston Churchill, mainly because Dr. Ronald Fieve, author of *Moodswing,* mentioned that Churchill exhibited many of the characteristics of a manic-depressive person. How could such a person become one of the greatest men of our time, and yet have had a mental illness? I wanted to know how he structured and lived his life. I also thought Churchill had integrity. His life was filled with both despair and greatness, but he lived what he believed in.

During this period I also became involved with the men's movement. I wanted a better understanding of who I was as a male person as opposed to just a human being. I felt there were distinct differences in the area of gender, and the men's movement offered an opportunity to address the subject of maleness directly. There also seemed to be some difference of opinion among men themselves as to what constituted the men's movement. I decided to find out for myself what I could learn from it.

CHAPTER 14

On Being Human and Male

Participating in the men's movement was a refreshing experience for me. I gained social, psychic, and intellectual benefits from it, although I did not become a prominent actor in the movement. I had the opportunity to be around other men in a setting of friendship and noncompetitiveness. We created a space in which we could discuss issues that are infrequently addressed in society. It was a time for going within yourself to question and to feel that part of yourself that had been beaten down time after time. There was opportunity to explore different aspects of who you were as a man, and to discuss these aspects with others, who would listen and in turn relate their own experiences. In this way the web of understanding is woven.

The different perspectives offered by the people I met in the men's movement were invaluable to me. I learned to see myself from the viewpoints of at least four generations: my grandfathers', my father's, my own, and my future sons'. The larger vision replaced my present-oriented tunnel vision with a perspective that spanned four generations. I began to understand how my world had been shaped by the ones who came before—the ascendants—and how I was shaping it for the generations to come. I had noticed, in my reading, a tendency for each generation to blame the previous generation for the state of things, and there is some truth to that charge. But if we use our unhappiness with the status quo to destroy what the ascendants have created, we merely continue in the same vicious circle. If, however, we seek to understand why they did the things they did, we can begin to heal not only ourselves but past and future generations as well.

In the time since the Industrial Revolution, Americans have undergone a significant shift in values. We have become a society that strives for material gain at any cost. That cost has become painfully evident in the mass destruction that has followed in the wake of "progress." We have put a man on the moon but wiped out the forests of the world. We have designed an artificial heart but produced acid rain. We invented plastics, useful in countless ways, that now pollute and strangle our oceans. We have built a Tower of Babel, never considering the inevitable fall. That fall has already occurred and is evident in overcrowded prisons, the high rates of suicide and drug and alcohol abuse, fighting around the globe, and the destruction of our planet.

The men's movement hopes to redress some of these problems by encouraging personal responsibility. Personal responsibility starts with the individual, starts with you and me taking responsibility in our own lives. If we cannot take responsibility in our own lives, we cannot possibly take responsibility in the world at large. And, step by step, or "bucket by bucket," in Robert Bly's words, we can eventually come to a new understanding of manliness, one that eschews dominance and money-making in favor of the stance of a guardian: guardians not only of our lives but of the planet. Sam Keen in *Fire in the Belly* says it this way:

> Our task is to create a new vision of manliness in a culture that no longer believes in saints, divinely revealed ideals, or absolute values. We are trapped within modern, masculine madness and can't find an exit; we live in the urgency of the moment, captive to quarterly profit reports and the trends of the day, but desperately needing an opening beyond the present to something that offers us more hope and dignity.

The men's movement, I discovered, is an inside movement: not in the sense of selfishness but of self-reflection. The men's movement does not reject society but instead strives for a much-needed re-evaluation of society. The hoped-for result is a greater active role in society, not a lesser role. The men's movement does not want to stifle our ignorant behavior of the past. Rather, it offers time in which the immature attitudes and actions of the male psyche can be observed, honored, and matured. A time for learning, a time for honoring our ignorance.

I would like to say something about the word ignorance. Ignorance has acquired an unfortunate meaning in our society. Call someone ignorant and you will know what I mean. Ignorance is defined as "lacking in knowledge." But ignorance has a valor of its own. It is a tool we can use to begin to know things. Sadly, we have become so sensitive to ridicule that we do not allow our ignorance to surface. If we hide our ignorance, we hinder our growth process. Every aspect of man holds a gift for us. If we honor our ignorance, it can open doors to knowledge. As Sam Keen writes in *Fire in the Belly,*

> Legend has it that the Delphic Oracle proclaimed there was no living man wiser than Socrates, but she also said that if he were wiser than others it was only because he knew his ignorance and was willing to keep searching for knowledge.

One of the ways in which the men's movement travels is through mythological stories of the past. By understanding the symbolic meanings of myths, we can draw parallels with our own lives that will allow us to explore areas of our psyche we find difficult to clothe in words. Myths offer meanings for our personal lives but, more important, they provide a structure that transcends the personal and places it within a broader historical and spiritual context. In particular, the heroic trial of myths has seen new life in the men's movement. In modern terms, the heroic trial involves coming to psychological maturity. This trial is offered to everyone. How we make use of it depends on whether we can undergo the necessary transformation of consciousness. To explain what I mean, and how myths are used by the men's movement, I will turn to the words of Joseph Campbell.

THE HEROIC JOURNEY OF INITIATION

Joseph Campbell, who died in 1987, was one of the foremost authorities on mythology. In a series of interviews on PBS with Bill Moyers, later published as *The Powers of Myth,* we are introduced to the different functions of myths and how they can help us see ourselves in modern society. The following dialogue is from an episode called "The Hero's Adventure":

Moyers: So in all of these cultures, whatever the local costume the hero might be wearing, what is the deed?

Campbell: Well, there are two types of deed. One is the physical deed, in which the hero performs a courageous act in battle or saves a life. The other kind is a spiritual deed, in which the hero learns to experience the supernormal range of human spiritual life and then comes back with a message.

The usual hero adventure begins with someone from whom something has been taken, or feels there's something lacking in the normal experiences available or permitted to the members of his society. This person then takes off on a series of adventures beyond the ordinary, either to recover what has been lost or to discover some life-giving elixir. It's usually a cycle, a going and a returning.

But the structure and something of the spiritual sense of this adventure can be seen already anticipated in the puberty or initiation rituals of early tribal societies, through which a child is compelled to give up its childhood and become an adult—to die, you might say, to its infantile personality and psyche and come back as a responsible adult. This is a fundamental psychological transformation that everyone has to undergo. We are in a childhood dependency under someone's protection and supervision for some fourteen to twenty-one years—and if you're going on for your Ph.D., this may continue to perhaps thirty-five. You are in no way a self-responsible, free agent, but an obedient dependent, expecting and receiving punishments and rewards. To evolve out of this position of psychological immaturity to the courage of self-responsibility and assurance requires a death and a resurrection. That's the basic motif of the hero's journey—leaving one condition and finding the source of life to bring you forth into a richer or mature condition.

Moyers: So even if we happen not to be heroes in the general sense of redeeming society, we still

> have to take that journey inside ourselves,
> spiritually and psychologically.

Campbell: That's right.

As Moyers pointed out during this interview, we can all be heros in some aspect of our lives. This idea has been a touchstone in the men's movement. Another theme pertinent to the men's movement is the lack of societal backing to aid the passage from a boy's psyche to a man's psyche. The initiation rituals of early tribal societies, whereby a child was ushered into an adult role, have been done away with in our society. Instead, we experience a constant struggle to grow from boyhood to manhood. This initiation process should have been the responsibility of our fathers and grandfathers, but for whatever reason, it did not take place. Initiation rituals also help the individual see that he is part of a larger history: However personally we feel our joys and sufferings, those feelings are not unique to us. Others have experienced the same feelings, for the same reasons, in the past; yet others will do so in the future. As Robert Bly has pointed out, all humans inhabit a story that includes but is much larger than our personal lives.

Within this general framework the "spiritual deed" of the hero referred to by Campbell has a special meaning for me. In a significant sense, I am trying to "come back with a message" from an adventure I was "thrown into." Learning about myths and the roles they play helped me understand that although I have passed through the greater part of my adventure alone, spiritual adventuring is common to millions of people. Without initiation rites to aid us in developing psychological maturity, growing up has become, in modern society, a major adventure. The question is whether we rise to the adventure and its tests and learn something from them, or seek to avoid them.

Later in the interview Moyers asked about the function of the ordeal or trial in myths:

Moyers: What's the significance of the trials, and tests, and ordeals of the hero?

Campbell: If you want to put it in terms of intention, the trials are designed to see to it that the intending hero should be really a hero. Is he really a match for this task? Can he overcome the dangers? Does he have the courage, the knowledge, the capacity, to enable him to survive?

Moyers: In this culture of easy religion, cheaply achieved, it seems to me we've forgotten that all three of the great religions teach that the trials of the hero journey are a significant part of life, that there's no reward without renunciation, without paying the price. The Koran says, "Do you think that you shall enter the Garden of Bliss without such trials as came to those who passed before you? And Jesus said in the gospel of Matthew, "Great is the gate and narrow is the way which leadeth to life, and few there be to find it." And the heroes of the Jewish tradition undergo great tests before they arrive at their redemption.

Campbell: If you realize what the real problem is— losing yourself, giving yourself to some higher end, or to another—you realize that this itself is the ultimate trial. When we

159

Moyers: quit thinking primarily about ourselves and our own self-preservation, we undergo a truly heroic transformation of consciousness. And what all myths have to deal with is transformations of consciousness of one kind or another. You have been thinking one way, now you have to think a different way.

Moyers: How is consciousness transformed?

Campbell: Either by the trials themselves or by illuminating revelations. Trials and revelations are what it's all about.

As Campbell pointed out, a key part of the heroic trial involves a transformation of consciousness. Through myths, we are instructed to give ourselves to "some higher end," to place ourselves in service to a higher cause that will help us pass the trials. In Jungian terms, this is known as recentering the ego. And when this is accomplished we will experience a transformation of consciousness.

When we allow myths to enter the fertile soil of our unconscious being, we create the possibility for inward growth. Each of us can relate many different areas of our lives to the mythical stories of the past. Myths do not so much supply us with meaning, although they can do that, as they provide a structure into which we can plug our own experiences. By seeing ourselves as mythic actors we can develop a broader perspective and a better understanding of ourselves in our struggle with life. Physically, mentally, and emotionally, life has always been the same, down through the ages.

CHAPTER 15

Boundaries and Transitions

During my first year in therapy I started to understand how different attitudes can alter an individual's behavior in one way or another. These attitudes can come from a myriad of different sources, such as the family, religious training, friends, television, and so on. I started to learn about the structure I grew up in, and how it influenced my thought processes. I was then able, over a period of time, to begin noticing how I responded to someone, and then to decide whether that response was mature. I learned different ways of responding, ways that were more appropriate than the ones I had learned as a child. Now, as I began to replace immature responses with mature responses, what I found really interesting was that I could also begin to see whether or not the other person was responding immaturely or maturely. What a wonderful insight to have gained!

When I first met Natalie H. Rogers, my therapist, one of the questions I wanted answered was where my thoughts, feelings, and emotions began and ended as opposed to other people's thoughts, feelings, and emotions. I will give an example of what I mean. If you are around someone who is experiencing a strong emotion, such as grief, you may also experience grief. Or, if someone is experiencing great joy, you may also begin to feel joy within yourself. These feelings, although first experienced by someone else, trigger the same feelings in you. I wanted to know whether those feelings were only those of the other person, whether they were mine and had been triggered by the other person, or whether they were a combination of both. And if they were a combination, at what point did my feelings end and the other person's feelings begin?

This was explained to me in terms of boundaries. I did not understand boundaries at all. What were they? What were they for? How should they be defended? This was all new to me, and it took some time to learn.

In learning about boundaries, I was given two exercises to perform. In the first exercise I could not give money to anyone who begged. I had mentioned during a therapy session that I sometimes felt I gave money to people just to get rid of them, not because I wanted to help them. My therapist insisted this was a boundary issue and gave me direct instructions not to give money to any beggars at all.

Over a period of several weeks I began to understand the point of this exercise. My therapist had given me an immovable boundary that I was not allowed to cross by giving money, nor could it be crossed by those asking for money. They had a right to ask, but that was all. My first experience in refusing money was, I felt, one of self-empowerment. When I was asked for money by someone to whom I did not want to give money anyway, I refused by telling myself I was doing my homework. I "borrowed" the power from the exercise because I did not possess it myself. By borrowing the power to refuse money, I could begin to feel the inner struggles of my consciousness. Guilt surfaced. Issues of morality surfaced. Attitudes came to light that were in conflict with one another and kept me in conflict with myself. On the other hand, when someone to whom I really wanted to give money asked for it, but I could not give the money because I was observing the boundary, the psychic process was the same. And not only did the guilt feelings and morality issues arise, I also felt anger—an anger that wanted to attach itself to someone or something.

Through this fairly simple exercise of creating a boundary, I was freed to focus on what was happening in my psyche. I began to see elements from my Catholic upbringing directing my actions in life. Guilt was pushing me around, consciously and unconsciously. Anger was running around inside me, searching for expression. Here again, I was able to identify learned behaviors that were inappropriate for my present life situation. These learned behaviors were for the most part unconscious: unconscious because they had not been taught to me directly but had been impressed upon me through daily living. Many unsaid things, many ways of being, are incorporated into the Christian way of life. Once I became aware that these things existed and ruled my behavior, I could bring them forward into the light of my consciousness. After that it would be only a matter of time before I could "rewire" myself.

By not giving money to anyone who asked, I was able to form a boundary that I was consciously aware of and that I could choose to cross or defend, depending on how I felt. Crossing the boundary became my choice, free from any entanglement of guilt or morality issues.

In my second exercise in forming boundaries, I was instructed to screen all incoming telephone calls with the answering machine. My therapist explained it this way: Why do we let anyone just jump into our lives whenever they decide they want to talk to us? You might be sleeping or doing something you don't want to be taken away from. I could see her point, but I thought it was rude not to answer the phone when you were home. And people might think I was avoiding them. People will think what they want to think, she said; and as far as being rude is concerned, that is just coming out of your upbringing. Screening calls has nothing to do with being rude. So I was instructed to screen all calls. If I wanted to talk to callers, I would have to call them back after they had left a message. Just as in the experience of withholding money, feelings of guilt and questions of right and wrong surfaced. I allowed myself to feel them without acting on them. After a while I was again able to see how certain characteristics of the psyche act on us consciously and unconsciously. These were ingenious exercises that were simple but led me to deep insights into how my mind was reacting to situations, and why. They helped me understand how my mind had been educated. By setting and observing boundaries I was able to relate effects to causes from the position of an observer, and without having to pass a judgment on the rightness or wrongness of the boundary action.

The exercises in setting boundaries also underscore the kind of relationship I developed with my therapist. At different times during therapy I found myself oscillating between enlightenment and misery, between understanding why I experienced certain things in a particular way and being overwhelmed by emotions that poured out of me. At these times I relied heavily on my therapist. I trusted her to know what was happening, and I followed her instructions. The exercises in setting boundaries were just one of the ways in which she helped me out of impasses. Often, in therapy, I felt that I was getting nowhere and just wasting my time. But at other times I knew I had progressed light years from where I had started.

STRESS RELEASE

The process of growth requires that the individual actually experience his or her pain. It requires the individual to be not only the observer but also the observed, the participant. The individual must experience the feelings of anger, hate, or remorse. By allowing yourself to feel these emotions you can release yourself from the bonds you have created for yourself. In an important way, personal growth is connected to acknowledging feelings and allowing yourself to feel them, without being led around by them.

Acknowledging and experiencing feelings is a form of stress release, but this release of stress may be manifested as psychological disturbances. These psychological disturbances can be confusing. People experiencing such disturbances question whether they are "sick"; others are happy to tell them they are sick. But psychological disturbances can accompany spiritual growth without in any way being a manifestation of an organic disorder. The release of stress and the subsequent resetting of the individual's emotional and psychic compass may be inherently tied to the development of spirituality.

The concept of stress release and its relationship to psychological disturbances was at first difficult for me to understand. During this time I came across an interesting book called *Growing Sane,* by James Stallone and Sy Migdal. This book deals with the psychological disturbances that accompany the growth of consciousness. The authors develop the position that an individual's growth process involves both the accumulation of stress and the release of stress. They focus on the release of stress as a means for personal growth, particularly addressing the difference between the growth process and psychosis. People experiencing confusion, doubt, and depression, wrote Stallone and Migdal, might in a cursory view appear to be in the grip of a deep psychological disturbance, potentially psychosis, for the symptoms of psychosis and the symptoms of a personal growth crisis can look the same on the surface. But there is an important difference between psychosis and a growth crisis. That difference, according to Stallone and Migdal, is an awareness of what is going on while the disturbance is taking place:

> [T]ruly psychotic . . . persons are not able to tell the difference between themselves and the symptoms; in a sense they become the symptoms. Psychotic persons are by no means detached observers, watching themselves play an unpleasant role. In fact, truly psychotic persons are so overcome and overshadowed by their symptoms that they frequently do not know enough even to seek help from their suffering.

A person who is not psychotic but is merely experiencing a growth crisis, on the other hand, does assume the stance of detached observer. Such individuals seem to be standing outside themselves, watching the emotional excursions that are taking place.

An awareness of some disturbances taking place was exactly my experience of hypomania. In all four episodes, I was able to sit back and watch my mind working. And following out Stallone and Migdal's thinking, if the hypomania did not progress to mania, it could be considered part of the growth process.

Awareness, then, etches the thin boundary between psychosis and growth. My experiences allow me to understand this difference. But logic and my heart urge me to push this understanding further. If hypomania is one way in which personal growth makes itself known, then crossing the boundary dividing sanity from insanity may also become a tool in a growth process that is strictly spiritual. A manic episode can be frightening indeed, for the psyche is not prepared for the accelerated pace of events or for the revelations of the mind's powers. But just as in learning anything else, you must be allowed to push beyond the known limits in order to fully understand what it is you are dealing with. Crossing the limits is not mandatory, but it can lead to a fuller understanding.

Let us return now from the outermost limits to the ordinary limits that constrain our personal growth. The course of personal growth often involves giving up old, comfortable ways of dealing with the world and advancing into unknown territory. A characteristic of growth is passage: entering and completing a transitional state, crossing a bridge. Stallone and Migdal emphasize that these passages and transitions result naturally from the growth of consciousness and should not be dismissed as signs of insanity. People enduring transitional states as part of the growth process have not lost contact with reality, as truly psychotic people have. Their very awareness of the psychic changes taking place places them firmly within the context of reality.

The language of transition suggested by Stallone and Migdal drives deeply to the heart of my concern, which is to separate the varieties of experience leading to spiritual growth from actual, persistent mental illness. Particularly in hypomania, the term "transitional state" would be less damaging than the term "mental illness," for the latter locks you in a box you can never hope to get out of. The word "transitional" allows the individual to understand that he or she is having a temporary experience. The medical profession, in a hurried way, designates mania, hypomania, and all similar experiences "mental illness," and the label sticks for life. The problem is compounded by the subjective mind of the newly designated "patient," which is powerfully open to suggestion. The individual, having received the imprint of another's mind (the doctor's mind), will accept hypomania as a negative experience, thus creating a vicious circle. Replacing "mental illness" with "transitional state" would not only alleviate the fear of people experiencing heightened psychic or spiritual states but would also allow them to regard such experiences as positive, or at least non-negative.

The two ideas from *Growing Sane* that I have discussed so far—awareness as the boundary separating the psychological disturbances of growth from true mental illness, and the concept of growth as marked by transitional phases—prepare the stage for a discussion of stress release, which is the focus of the book. They are the hallmarks of a "purification process" whereby the self relieves itself of stress. The notion of purification involved in stress release is a radical extension of psychological theory and one that is worth examining in detail.

"Ordinary psychology," the authors point out, "is used to dealing with persons who have accumulated such an abundance of stress in their lives that they are incapable of living under the strain. Disturbances that result from over-accumulation of stress generally lead to what we call mental illness." This is a fairly standard sort of statement in the psychological literature: too much stress causes problems, which we label mental illness. Relieving stress re-sets the body's mechanism on its usual course. But note there is no progress in this course of events. The subject simply moves in cycles of very short excursions, often starting over from the same place every time.

In spiritual growth, by contrast, the situation is not one of stress causing problems, but just the reverse: the release of stress creates psychological disturbances. The problems encountered on the path to enlightenment, Stallone and Migdal say, result from the release of stress: "The body and the mind are purifying themselves of stress, sometimes in a faster and more intense way than we know how to handle." With these words the authors stand conventional psychology on its head, reversing cause and effect. Such a reversal is not always available. It accompanies the growth of spiritual awareness. If there is no growth, there is no purification. Stress remains the daily diet. But if there is spiritual growth, the purification, the release of stress, can be explosive.

Stallone and Migdal's revision of the idea of stress fits in well with my own views on manic-depression. My first three experiences were all stress related. The first episode, I was told, was precipitated by an accumulation of stressful events. The second occurred during a course designed to release stress, and the third similarly came hard on the heels of stress-releasing exercises. The fourth experience I also discovered, much later, to be associated with stress release, but in a different way: It came about in part by my practicing yoga, which, as I did not know but was to find out, is a stress-releasing form of exercise.

In light of what I learned from Stallone and Migdal about stress release, I must now ask myself, Did the psychological disturbances I experienced during mania result from a build-up of stress, as standard psychology would have it, or did they result from a release of stress in the form of purification? The key seems to be awareness. During my first episode I was ignorant of all ideas about spiritual development, and in all honesty I must regard this episode as a standard textbook case: increasing stress brought on severe problems. The treatment and its results were equally devoid of any shadow of enlightenment. I went home from the hospital on lithium, returned to school, and did as I was told.

But the subsequent episodes occurred in a climate of increasing psychic awareness on my part. They were qualitatively different, and they occurred in a different context as well. I was involved in stress-releasing exercises and plunged beyond the limits envisioned by the people who designed the exercises. I had engaged in the release of stress and got in over my head. The purification that my being wanted happened in "a faster and more intense way" than I or anyone else knew how to handle. In performing stress release work I opened myself to experiences that temporarily overwhelmed me, but I was able to observe myself throughout and to learn from these experiences.

Finding the Self

In *Growing Sane,* Stallone and Migdal examine the various stages of the growth of consciousness. Before the growth of consciousness can occur, however, development of the individual, or ego development, must have sufficiently matured to provide a good grounding for the pursuit of higher awareness. This area of growth is traditionally known as developmental psychology. The importance of ego development can be inferred from the following passage:

> You must establish yourself as a separate, independent, individuated adult before permanent stabilization in enlightenment or higher consciousness is possible. You need to go through certain stages in order to pass from childhood-adolescence to adulthood. If not, you will be stuck defending yourself from the fear of abandonment and subsequent depression associated with being on your own.

Stallone and Migdal divide the areas of growth considered in developmental psychology into "physical, intellectual, social, moral, financial/vocational, and ego/emotional." There is a clear connection here with the guidelines for attaining spiritual growth, which emphasize the importance of development of your character, and also a clear connection with the issues that have arisen in the men's movement, specifically the need to advance into a mature, adult state from the immature, childlike state in which modern men find themselves trapped. Thus, the stages in ego development that prepare the ground for spiritual advancement apply both to the individual and to larger social groups. And third, I was interested to see that moral development is an important and defined stage in ego development. Improving one's moral character is an essential part of virtually all spiritual practices. In this fashion, our day-to-day personal development is inextricably linked to our hope for attaining a higher spiritual state.

In describing the growth of consciousness, Stallone and Migdal were influenced by the work of Roberto Assagioli, whose concept of the will I outlined briefly in Chapter 7. According to Stallone and Migdal, the growth of consciousness is marked by the following four phases:

1. Seeking
2. Temporary finding
3. Temporary losing
4. Intensification of finding and losing

In the "seeking" stage, an individual senses that there is something more to life than what he or she is experiencing—and goes looking for it. Many people turn to religion in this stage. Others become involved in self-help groups or enter therapy. There are no temporal limits to the seeking stage. It may last a short time or continue throughout life; it may come to you in youth or wait for you in your later years. It is a period of confusion and discontent. Needless to say, it is not a very comfortable stage.

In the second stage, "temporary finding," the individual experiences that part of himself that is his true Self. The individual glimpses "oneness," a profound experience. But with this glimpse comes confusion and crisis. In the first manifestation of transcendental consciousness, Stallone and Migdal write, "the Self bursts through the shell of ignorance and stress, and the experience is exhilarating—charged with energy." The intensity of the first experience can be very mild or overpowering, depending on the predilection of the individual. If it is the latter, the experience of the deepest

Self may be accompanied by a huge release of stress and the discharge of pent-up emotions. The experience can feel overwhelming, even uncontrollable. But in either case, whether the experience is mild or overpowering, the revelation of the true Self exposes an ego that is wanting: it is in want of attention, approval, and affection.

Here we must stop for a moment and consider the ego self and the transcendental Self, and how the two can get along with each other. In the stage of finding, the higher Self, or "oneness," unveils some deficiencies in the ego self. The ego self wants love and attention, and to get these things it tries to rope in the higher Self. It tries to conflate the higher Self and the ego self and make them one, that one being the ego self. It is a characteristic of mania that the individual takes his higher Self to be his ego self, and acts accordingly. But the transcendental Self is an outward movement that resists the efforts of the ego self to diminish it. The person experiencing growth of consciousness finds his or her consciousness radiating outward. Intuition soars. The senses are more attuned to the environment and to other people. Perceptions become highly refined. These effects filter into and enhance the ego self, but the ego self in turn must continue its own maturation process, its own development, in order to provide a firm grounding for spiritual development to occur. This is where standard psychology and spirituality intersect. A person who has not matured in the usual psychological sense is insufficiently prepared to experience the transcendental Self in a productive way.

There are two "temptations," and two controls over those temptations, that can arise in the finding of the higher Self. The first temptation I have already mentioned: The ego self identifies the higher Self as itself. The result is megalomania, "an unrealistic notion of who and what you really are," in the words of Stallone and Migdal. The individual assumes a falsely inflated sense of self-importance. The second temptation is to get caught up in the by-products of finding the Self, in the wonderful intuitions and sharpened sense perceptions. The individual wallows in these by-products and may try to commercialize a gift of healing or the ability to see future events.

By remaining aware of the growth process, the individual can avoid these temptations and keep on track. There are also specific controls that can be put into place. *Meditations on the Tarot* recommends worship and work—ora et labora—as practical checks on the tendency toward megalomania. "Worship" in this case simply means that the individual acknowledges a higher goal, or a higher being, than his own puny existence. "Work" I interpret to mean in this context the grounding structure of what the self is capable of, or character development of the personal self. And arcing over these specific controls, an attitude of attention or awareness will always help the individual use the tools of worship and work to proceed along the course of spiritual development.

The third stage in the growth of consciousness is "temporary losing." In this stage the experience of temporary finding slowly fades. It is a stage of integration. The experience of the transcendental Self gradually infiltrates our personality, our physiology, our way of being and thinking about ourselves. Much of this infiltration or incorporation appears to go on at a subsurface or subconscious level. Stallone and Migdal explain the reason for this stage as the time needed by the nervous system to adjust to the shock of the finding stage. We can extend this observation in a general way: All new experiences take time to assimilate, to penetrate our being and do their work on multiple levels. The experience of the Self differs from other kinds of insights in that its affects are felt at all levels. It has the potential to revolutionize our lives.

From the spiritual point of view, the stage of temporary losing would seem to be a step backward, but in fact it is not a going backward. It is a stage of consolidation and reflection, which must take place before further advancement along the spiritual path can occur. This stage has its counterpart in the "gnosis" of Christian Hermeticism, the reflection on the pure act.

The last stage in the growth of consciousness is the stage of "intensification of finding and losing." This stage is an intensified reiteration of the second and third stages. With the initial break through our stress walls and the subsequent integration of the experience, we start a process that can continue in the same pattern, but at a faster pace. The growth process can continue, alternating periods of release of stress (finding) with periods of integration (losing).

In *Growing Sane,* Stallone and Migdal list several techniques that an individual can use in the growth process. These techniques are:

1. Intellectual understanding
2. Upliftment/reinforcement
3. Keeping a vision of the goal
4. Daily routine
5. "Feeling the body"
6. Intense physical exercise
7. Affirmations
8. Daily acts of the will
9. Interpersonal communication skills

Each of these techniques helps the individual build a solid foundation that can be used in the growth process. All deal with the individual's character traits. Unless a person is fully developed as a mature being, he or she will not be grounded enough to successfully grow spiritually.

Growing Sane provides a wonderful insight into the growth of consciousness by wedding spirituality to modern-day psychology. It helps people who are in the throes of psychological disturbances as a result of personal growth understand that these disturbances are not manifestations of mental illness. The distinction Stallone and Migdal draw between sanity and insanity has to do with awareness. I have found this discrimination very helpful. But my view pushes beyond this line into the realm of insanity. It begins where this book ends. In my experience, I have crossed the line dividing sanity from insanity three times, and in my view, what the authors say about psychological disturbances resulting from the growth of consciousness can apply equally well to the transitional stage of mania, even if the subject is not aware of the process taking place. Even the psychotically ill, deprived of an immediate awareness, may still participate in the growth of consciousness through their experiences. I agree entirely with Stallone and Migdal's work, as far as it goes. My work is the next step.

CHAPTER 17

Temperaments and Understanding

My years of intensive therapy bore fruit in a number of ways not directly connected to any problems I worked on with my therapist. One of the most important discoveries I made during this period of personal growth was how my mind works in regard to assimilating information about my environment. It came about through my search for a career.

After I graduated from college, I found myself without direction. I was not overpoweringly drawn to enter any one particular field. In the decade following graduation I did what I wanted to do, which was to learn about my mind. I had no desire to accumulate large amounts of money, no desire to scale the corporate ladder. I worked at minor jobs that gave me the time and the resources to pursue my quest, but none of these jobs particularly defined my relationship to the world.

After I had been in therapy for about a year, my therapist suggested it was time for me to find a path that would allow me to enter society as a functional part of the system, a path that would also allow my personal identity to "breathe." Finding my niche in the workplace, she said, would help create a balance in my life. Without a career to direct my energies into, my life in other areas would always be unbalanced. I would continue to lean on these other areas for the support and fulfillment it was not within their power or structure to give. And in so doing I would create a stressful situation that would always keep me feeling conflicted.

It was a difficult process to begin. It seemed I had always been searching unconsciously in this area, with poor or no results. I also felt some pressure to choose a path I could follow. Just as in high school, when I was told to pick a career, I felt at a loss and quite helpless. My therapist finally found someone who had created a system that accommodated itself to my specific needs. This person did not work in the usual manner of career counselors. Instead of starting with my education, we began by inventorying all of my past work experiences, starting from the first, which was selling lemonade, to the present. We included all work, both paid and unpaid. With this inventory came a volume of questions concerning my likes and dislikes. I also had to write down the ten most rewarding experiences of my life. We were constructing a profile that would encompass all aspects of my personality, not forgetting the negative aspects. The process took months to complete. And it was during this process of personal research that I came across a book that gave me an in-depth understanding of how my mind functioned. *Please Understand Me,* by David Keirsey and Marilyn Bates, provided an important insight into how I think and process information presented to me.

I had always assumed that the human mind was basically the same for everyone—that everyone's thought processes followed the same patterns, and that the only difference lay in the level of intelligence. I believed that people presented with the same stimulus would respond in the same way, and that would be the way that I responded. Reading *Please Understand Me* showed me that in fact, other people are much more likely to respond in a way that is different from one's own way of responding. For people are inherently different from one another, and the differences cannot be altered (although they may be camouflaged) by education, training, or any other social or behavioral factor. Once I learned this, I was able to understand why I had had particular problems all my life in certain areas involving other people. It was as if I had been forced to spend my life in a square hole, only to find out I was a round peg. Discovering I was a round peg dissipated much of the confusion surrounding my communications with other people. It was a powerful and freeing experience.

Please Understand Me deals with the character and temperament types of individuals. It proposes a model of four primary ways of thinking, with each mode divided into four subsets, for a total of sixteen categories altogether. The book's main theme is that people are inherently different from one another, but they are different in ways that fall into types or temperaments.

The historical roots to the idea of temperaments, according to the authors, reach as far back as Hippocrates, who divided human temperaments into choleric, phlegmatic, melancholic, and sanguine types. This idea of fundamentally different temperaments, first articulated twenty-five centuries ago, remained influential for some time, probably through Europe's Middle Ages. The Age of Enlightenment in Europe and the United States saw the flowering of democratic institutions and a corresponding fade in the idea of temperaments. If people are equal then they must be alike, it was thought. The leveling or amalgamation into one appeared to be complete with the appearance of Freud and the Viennese psychoanalytic school at the end of the nineteenth century. Freud believed that all humans operate from universal instincts which can be understood as different manifestations of Eros. These universal instincts, however they might be culturally expressed, become the Great leveler.

In the decades of Freud's mature work, others heeded the clarion call of "we are all alike," following out the idea of singular motaivation. Adler replaced Eros with the desire for power as the instinct motivating all humans. Sullivan replaced power with the instinct for social solidarity, and the Existentialists decided that the basic motivating instinct was the search for the Self. Regardless of which instinct happened to be valorized, each of these schools of thought held that the same primary instinct motivated all people, everywhere, at all times.

A notable exception to this trend of the universal instinct was Carl Jung. In 1920, Jung proposed that, although people may be driven by one or a multitude of instincts, no one instinct is more important than another. Instead, he saw people differing in innate preferences for how they function. The preference for a particular way of functioning is an unalterable characteristic that allows people to be understood as different types. In this way Jung invented "functional types" or "psychological types." Jung referred to these psychological types as archetypes.

Several other voices were raised in the mid-twentieth century, claiming either unity or multiplicity of motives in driving human behavior. When the dust settled, the two opposing schools of dynamic psychology and behavioral psychology appeared triumphant. Forgotten in the arguments over behaviors, interactions, ego development, the instincts, and so forth was the concept of different functional types. Jung was retired to library shelves as an interesting bit of literature.

The 1950s saw a revival of interest in Jung's psychological types and an extension of his theories. It happened almost accidentally. Isabel Myers and her mother, Katheryn Briggs, became interested in types, and together they devised the Myers-Briggs Type Indicator, a measure for assorting patterns of action into the sixteen basic types I mentioned earlier. The test has been widely used in psychological studies and has spearheaded an international renewal of interest in Jung's work on types. The test is all the more interesting because the sixteen Myers-Briggs types fall neatly into Hippocrates' four temperaments, thus bringing to full circle a multi-millennial investigation into human character.

This brief review of the history of temperament, which I have summarized from *Please Understand Me,* gave me a lot to think about. Once we understand that people have fundamentally different temperaments, we can begin to see our communications in a new light. It is no longer a case of "I'm right, you're wrong." Instead, there are two (or more) unique perceptions of the same stimulus. Rather than denying someone else's feelings, we can broaden our own understanding and increase our knowledge. Other people can become a source of wonder and intrigue, instead of being regarded as strange and nonsensible.

Jung constructed four dyads, or poles of behavior, from which all of the patterns of temperament can be assembled. These four dyads are not, of course, carved in stone. Each of us varies in the degree to which we prefer and express one or the other element of the dyad, but one aspect will always be dominant. The four dyads of preference are:

Preference for extraversion vs. introversion. A person who prefers extroversion is more likely to find a source of energy in other people, while a person who has a preference for introversion is more likely to retire into solitude to recover energy.

Preference for intuition vs. sensation. A practical person has a greater natural preference for sensation, whereas an innovative person is more apt to think and act intuitively.

Preference for thinking vs. feeling. Jung described a person who makes decisions on an impersonal basis as a thinking type, and a person who makes decisions on a personal basis a feeling type.

Preference for judging vs. perceiving. A person who prefers closure to keeping options open is a judging type. A person who likes to keep options open is a perceiving type.

The four temperaments represent an assemblage of different groupings from these four dyads. To make the temperaments easier to remember, Keirsey and Bates in *Please Understand Me* assigned them the names of the Greek gods, for certain features of the temperaments match quite closely the attributes of the gods:

Apollonian—Intuitive, feeling
Dionysian—Sensation, perception
Promethean—Intuitive, thinking
Epimethean—Sensation, judging

According to the ancient Greek myths, the authors wrote, "Apollo was commissioned to give man a sense of spirit, Dionysus to teach man joy, Prometheus to give man science, and Epimetheus to convey a sense of duty. . . . Who worships Apollo (spirit) does not worship Prometheus (science) and who desires Dionysian joy (or release) is not content with Epimethean duty. We see that the four temperaments are different from each other in very fundamental ways."

After taking the Myers-Briggs Type Indicator test, I found that my score put me in the category of the Prometheus temperament: introverted, intuitive, thinking, and judging. In the Greek myth it was Prometheus, a Titan who sided with Zeus in the war against the Titans and a very wise god, who, against the wishes of Zeus, went to the sun and stole fire. That fire he bestowed on man, giving him life. Although Prometheus was punished by Zeus for this act, he became a symbol of the fight against injustice and a true authority of power.

Prometheans, evidently, make up a smallish part of the population—only about twelve percent, according to Keirsey and Bates. They live as aliens on their own planet, surrounded by Dionysian and Epimethean types. In the home, a Promethean is lucky to have one parent who is another Promethean. In character traits, Prometheans are fascinated by the power of understanding and predicting nature that is the heartbeat of science ("Scratch a [Promethean], find a scientist"). A Promethean is also addicted to acquiring knowledge ("He ever attempts, in his Promethean way, to breathe a fire of understanding into whatever area he considers his domain") and to developing competence. Indeed, competence seems to be the end to which power and knowledge are used by the Promethean, and that competence—skills, abilities, ingenuity—must constantly be retested under different circumstances.

As I read about the Promethean temperament, I began to realize that everything I had done with my adult life was wholly in accordance with my temperament. A person with a Promethean temperament is serious about knowledge; he needs to know. I had always wondered why I was determined not to accept answers that seemed illogical. I had—and have—a drive to explore thoroughly areas of ignorance, especially areas that pertain to my own life.

Reading about the different temperaments also helped me understand why I sometimes encountered difficulties in everyday communications with other people. My thought processes really were different from theirs, and their thought processes were different from mine. Looking back, I could see that instances of confusion or misunderstanding in my life arose not because one party or the other was right or wrong, but because people simply think in different ways. When I add to this the immaturity of some parts of my character, I could understand why people perceived me in the way that they did.

This understanding was so powerful, it was as if someone had pulled a sheet off my head. I started to understand some things that had always before been incomprehensible. In my youth, for example, I was frequently questioned why I was doing something that I thought was perfectly logical. It was as if no one could see what I was doing. This happened so often that by the time I got to high school I had developed the perfect response, one that cut off all further dialogue. Instead of trying to give an explanation that would always fall short, I would say, "Because I am Bob Kelly," and that would be the end of it. It got even funnier after my first hospitalization. When someone in my family told me I was doing something crazy, I would say, "So I have been told"—again, a response that derailed further comment. These are but a few examples of the exasperation, confusion, and outright misunderstanding that dogged my days. I can now see that I did my part in exasperating and confusing other people.

The subject of communication, language, and thought processes continued to intrigue me for some time. After finishing *Please Understand Me,* I found another book, *You Just Don't Understand,* by Deborah Tannen, that describes the different conversational styles used by the different sexes. This book offers a different cut through the communicative difficulties that can beset people. It has made me more attuned to the nuances of everyday communication and the confusion that can arise if one ignores differences in how people speak and process information from their environment.

Much of this new information took time to assimilate. At first I simply had to become aware that people think and understand things differently, then I could use this knowledge to improve my own communication and understanding of what other people were saying. I'd like to draw a parallel with the awareness that Stallone and Migdal say is a necessary part of maturing psychically. Total awareness does not come overnight, but if a person can become aware of the process he or she is involved in, that individual is in a position of command instead of in a situation that commands the individual. Once I learned how to observe how I communicated, it was within my power to change my communications for the better, instead of being buffeted by misunderstandings.

The Uses of Imagination

In *The Master Mind,* the nineteenth-century writer Theron Dumont described the imagination as a tool that uses the information supplied by memory to advance our self-knowledge. When accessed with meaningful desire, imagination can be a powerful constructive force. But when accessed without will or intent to guide it into the work of increasing our self-knowledge, imagination can be like a fire that burns out of control. It usurps the position that action should rightfully occupy with "idle day dreams and vain fanciful flights of the imagination," in Dumont's words. It is no longer available as a tool that we can use to assist our personal growth.

The role of the imagination has continued to fascinate modern psychologists. It is a part of mental functioning that can never be directly interrogated but is quite obviously capable of bearing the enormous trust of helping us to interpret information from our environment and to develop psychically. Modern psychologists share with Dumont the view that the imagination can be used beneficially as an active force. They also recognize that unbridled imagination has the negative potential of alienating us from everyday reality in an unsatisfying way. Modern psychologists differ from those of Dumont's day chiefly in their description of the imagination as a medium rather than a force. Imagination mediates between the ego and the unconscious, between the human and the divine, between the known and the unknown. As a medium, imagination is most often referenced in the psychology literature in studies on ego psychology, for it seems to be a powerful tool for growth and one that most people can access easily. In this chapter, which is really a prelude to the next, I summarize some of the modern thinking on the imagination and use it as a vehicle for understanding my experience with mania.

In *Imagination as Space of Freedom,* the internationally renowned psychotherapist Verena Kast describes imagination as a "dialogue between the ego and the unconscious." Through this dialogue, she says, the individual's conscious can access a world of other possibilities other than what we have right now. The dialogue that is joined when imagination meets the quotidian serves as a bridge for creative transformations, allowing us to transform our lives in some way that we have imagined, or, alternatively, bringing the imagined within the compass of our grasp. It is the space where creative drives make themselves known and can be usefully directed.

In its farthest reach, Kast says, imagination is the expression of a basic human desire for something not just different but "utterly other": for the divine. Imagination can then be understood as a dialogue between the human and the divine, however we care to define divine. This dialogue allows us to shape the divine, to bring it within conscious perception, even as we approach it. This is perhaps the pinnacle of the "creative transformation" that imagination can supply.

In its more usual function, according to Kast, imagination helps us organize our emotions and thoughts. It emplaces a balance in our lives by helping us interpret information we receive from our surroundings and from our psyche, and by helping us find solutions to everyday problems. Everyone uses imagination to some degree every day to find solutions that fit the context of reality. The less information that is available, the more we will rely on imagination to compose an "unambiguous picture" (Kast's words) of the situation. The unambiguous picture helps us retain an inner equilibrium, deal with anxiety, and master a difficult problem. In this way, imagination becomes a midwife to the creative processing of information.

Kast identifies two situations in which imagination can exceed our ability to use it well. The first case again has to do with processing information. If we are in a psychic state that restricts our ability to receive and process information, whether that information is about our emotions or our environment, the imaginary construct balloons and replaces any actual perception we have of the situation. Kast gives as an example total rage, which feeds on imagination and shuts the gate to actuality. The imaginary construct becomes the new reality. Imagination is still used to creatively transform the situation, but in a negative way, for its linking function to actuality is overridden.

In the second case, the individual's desire for something "utterly other" may become so strong that it silences the dialogue between the world of imagination and the world of reality. The individual enters wholly into the "other world" and lives there for a time. This ability has been used fruitfully by rare individuals, chiefly mystics and the ecstatic poets, who have returned to actuality transformed and able to relate their experiences. Most of us do not have this ability or cannot use it; we bow before fear and difficulty. But we can still use the imagination to develop our egos without having to seek the ultimate other. Remember that Kast describes imagination as a dialogue between the ego and the unconscious, the known and the unknown. The space where this dialogue takes place, where the ego is introduced to something new, which it can then pursue, is the space of freedom. We are most creative when we are in this space, and most able to make progress spiritually.

Many ideas from Kast's work seem to tie in to my own experiences. During the psychotic phases of my manic episodes, as I have related, I was lost in a world of imagination. I was a "wizard's wizard"—the best of the best. I was subject to the megalomanic delusions that psychotic people occasionally suffer from in thinking they are all-powerful. I addressed other people as "God," depending on the degree of authority they seemed to have. If was as if my mind, unable to process information from my environment in an appropriate way, relied wholly on the imagination to construct a conceptual picture of the universe. This picture I could hold onto. It supplied me with some sort of mental equilibrium, an interpretive grid through which I could somehow make sense of the world. It was a wholly "other" experience. Yet it seems to me that even in this unusual psychic state, my imagination did not fail in its dialogic or linking function, for it made available to my conscious mind certain extraordinary—mystical, if you will—experiences I could not otherwise achieve.

Kast understands imagination as a prerequisite for mystical experiences. Because the imagination opens a dialogue between the conscious and the unconscious, it can bring home to our conscious things previously unglimpsed. It is a tool that can be used to formulate the pure mystical experience so that it can be understood. This concept is addressed more explicitly in Christian Hermeticism, which tells us that "the pure act in itself cannot be grasped; it is only its reflection which renders it perceptible or understandable. . . ." In other words, it is through the reflection of the mystical (unconscious) experience in the conscious mind that the unknown can become known. Christian Hermeticism believes that the reflection of the pure act becomes perceptible in the mind through analogy: The reflection is like the pure act, but not it exactly. Modern psychology now seems to be suggesting that analogy attains its efficacy from imagination, the imagination that opens the dialogue between the conscious and the unconscious.

The difference between the pure act, or the pure experience, and its reflection in the mind I could use to understand my experiences of mania. As I see it, during mania the doors to my unconscious were wide open. They were open to some ultimate otherness that I had previously not even glimpsed. I experienced oneness and perfect harmony at a time when my psychological disturbances were so great I was labeled mentally ill. The pure experience left its reflection in my mind, awaiting only the direction of my will and desire to be put to use. The awakening I experienced will forever be part of my life. And all of the movements of this awakening—the descent into the unconscious, the experience of the unconscious, and the reflection of that experience in my mind—were framed by the functions of the imagination.

It was not enough for me simply to experience my imagination this way, of course. I had to think about those experiences consciously. In order for imagination to be used as a tool in psychological or spiritual growth, the ego must be actively involved. The conscious participation of the ego makes the connection between the conscious and the unconscious. The intertwined use of the ego and the imagination is sometimes referred to as "active imagination."

The active use of the imagination takes us back to Jung and Jungian archetypes. Jung spoke of the "vivification of interior images" and allowing them to have a voice. These interior images or figures occupy a deep layer of the psyche, which for present purposes we may take as the unconscious. In Jungian thought, the dialogue between the conscious and the unconscious, between the ego complex and the deepest psyche, is an active, "noisy" process. The ego and the interior images speak to each other, interrogating and analyzing each other. For the dialogue to be fruitful the ego must be wide awake and the individual must have some knowledge of and responsiveness to the interior images.

Jungian archetypes are images that sum up some relationship of the individual to himself and the world. They serve as models, not in the sense of patterns or something to be identified with, but in the sense of guidelines. The growth process occurs when we become aware of the images residing in our innermost psyche and discern whether those are fit, mature images or inappropriate for us. In the dialectic of ego and psyche, the archetypal image stands not as a referee but as a point of comparison. Once we become aware of the existence of these images and their functions, we can use them to grow emotionally, physically, and psychically into mature individuals.

The next chapter expands on the idea of the active imagination by visiting some Jungian-type images that have emerged with the men's movement. These images pertain specifically to the development of the male psyche, but the basic archetypal concepts and structure are the same for both sexes.

CHAPTER 19

From Boy to Man/ Archetypes for the Modern Age

During my involvement with the men's movement I came across a book on the aspects of mythical figures as they apply to the male psyche. *King, Warrior, Magician, Lover*, by Robert Moore and Douglas Gillette, provides a map of the male psyche through the use of archetypes. It has provided me with a structure I have been able to use in my own personal growth. It has also helped me understand the state of my ego during my manic episodes, which information I could then use to make some necessary adjustments.

King, Warrior, Magician, Lover arose out of the authors' concern for two vital issues. The first is the disappearance from our culture of rituals that would assist boys in making the transition from childhood to adulthood. The authors refer to these two states as the Boy psychology and the Man psychology. Everywhere we look, the authors say, the Boy psychology is evident in people who have chronologically reached adulthood. The Boy psychology is dominant. Its marks are easy to discern. These marks include violence against others (for true masculinity is not violent); passivity and weakness; the lack of ability to be effectual and creative in life; and the lack of ability to inspire creativity in others.

The second problem of concern to Moore and Gillette is the patriarchal society. "In our view," they write, "patriarchy is not the expression of deep and rooted masculinity . . . [but] the expression of the immature masculine." Patriarchy flourishes in a society stuck in the Boy psychology. It represents the negative side of masculinity, the side that has failed in ego development even as men reach chronological adulthood. In the authors' words, "It expresses the stunted masculine, fixated at immature levels."

With these two ideas in mind, Moore and Gillette embark on a journey through the masculine self. The path transits the field of archetype psychology. According to the authors, "archetypes provide the very foundations of our behaviors—our thinking, our feeling, and our characteristic human reactions." In humans they may be instinctive patterns; Jung likened archetypes to instincts in other animals. Artists and religious prophets seem particularly aware of archetypes and able to use them to communicate in ways that words cannot.

In the Boy psychology there are four archetypes, the Divine Child, the Precocious Child, the Oedipal Child, and the Hero. As the boy matures psychologically, these archetypes are replaced by their counterparts in the Man psychology: the King, Magician, Lover, and Warrior. In essence an expansion of the Jungian archetypes—Moore is a trained Jungian analyst—these archetypes can be thought of as functional modes, innate preferences for how we think and conduct ourselves in the world. Thus, the Divine Child will always mature (if he does) into the King, the Precocious Child into the Magician, and so on. These archetypes are not mutually exclusive, however. Rather, the individual personality is composed of a different quantitative mix of all the types; but there is usually one archetype that each of us "lives" in. The issue of maturity at each stage is important, for without the full maturation of the archetypes in the Boy psychology, the archetypes of the Man psychology cannot be fully accessed. The Man psychology presupposes maturation of the Boy psychology. If the Boy psychology does not mature fully, the immature aspects of childhood will continue into adult life, finding an outlet for expression in what the authors refer to as the shadow forms of the adult psyche.

Moore and Gillette use the triangle as the symbol for the structure of an archetype. Four triangles, representing the four archetypes of the Boy psychology or the Man psychology, together form a four-sided pyramid whose apex represents the archetypes in their fullness. The apex may be thought of as the point where the different archetypes come together in an individual and are maintained in perfect balance; it is the ideal culmination of human development. At the base of each triangle lies a bipolar shadow where the archetype is expressed in its dysfunctional or shadow forms. The shadow forms indicate a lack of cohesion in the psyche, which the authors view as a symptom of inadequate development. The two sides of the bipolar shadow will coalesce into a unified whole as the boy or the man matures in his appropriate stage of development. The structure of the archetype, the triangle with its shadow forms, applies to both the Boy psychology and the Man psychology.

In the rest of this chapter I explain each of the archetypes in the Boy psychology and the Man psychology, both in the fullness of their positive qualities and in their shadow sides. I have personally found them very helpful in my own growth. Understanding the structure of the archetypal map would be sufficient for now, but the vividness of the archetypal images, which most of us can relate to through our own experiences, will help you remember the stages of the specific types.

THE BOY PSYCHOLOGY

The Divine Child

The first archetype in the Boy psychology is the Divine Child. The Divine Child represents the aspect of divinity we see in the newborn infant, an all-powerful innocence but at the same time a profound helplessness. These features are found in both the positive archetype and the shadow form.

On the positive side, according to Moore and Gillette, "This Divine Child within us is the source of life. It possesses magical, empowering qualities, and getting in touch with it produces an enormous sense of well-being, enthusiasm for life, and great peace and joy. . . ."

The shadow side of the Divine Child manifests as either the High Chair Tyrant or the Weakling Prince. If you have ever spent time around infants, you are probably aware of the High Chair Tyrant and how demanding this personality type can be. The High Chair Tyrant is arrogant (in the sense of hubris, or overwhelming pride), childish (in a negative way), and irresponsible. He does not face up even to his basic biological and psychological needs. In the psychology literature, this type is described as pathologically narcissistic. "The High Chair Tyrant needs to learn that he is not the center of the universe and that the universe does not exist to fulfill his every need, or, better put, his limitless needs, his pretensions to godhood. It will nurture him, but not in his form as God."

The other shadow form, the Weakling Prince, is the opposite of the High Chair Tyrant. This shadow side is expressed in passivity. The child withdraws from life, appearing to be helpless in the overpowering game of life.

Like the other archetypes, the archetype of the Divine Child with its shadow forms does not go away. It is always present in the personality type, but it can mature. Throughout life we are always accessing, in some way or another, the Boy archetype of our personality. Maturity lies in the appropriate use of that archetype. Once we see whether the positive archetype or its shadow form predominates in our life, we can begin to make the necessary adjustments to realign ourselves with the Divine Child.

For an adult man, accessing the positive archetype of the Boy psychology is easier said than done. We need to acknowledge it and admire it, but not identify with it. In the case of the Divine Child, acknowledging means loving and admiring "the creativity and beauty of this primal aspect of the masculine Self." If we do not connect with the creative, hopeful nature of this archetype, we will not be able to see the creative possibilities in life. In the adult man, the Divine Child stands for renewal and a quickening to life.

The Precocious Child

The archetype of the Precocious Child represents that part of the Boy psychology that seeks to know all the answers. This archetype brings into focus human curiosity and adventurous impulses. The Precocious Child in us "urges us to be explorers and pioneers of the unknown, the strange and mysterious."

The Precocious Child is concerned with both the world around us and the world within us. He is interested in why people, including himself, act the way they do. He investigates how and why he responds to people. He is likely to be introverted and reflective, and may exhibit unusual insight into hidden relations in things.

The shadow side of the Precocious Child manifests as the Know-It-All Trickster and the Dummy. The Know-It-All Trickster is the immature aspect of the child or man who refuses to accept responsibility for himself. He constantly attacks others as inferior. He manipulates others into believing him, then turns on them, making them out to be fools.

Just as the Precocious Child is curious and energetic, so too is the Know-It-All Trickster, but in the shadow form the energy is misdirected and immature. The Trickster is a fairly complex but also fairly common mode, and so we need to understand it. The curiosity that leads the Precocious Child to uncover some truth about the world can, in the Trickster, lead to lies, destruction, and hostility. Moore and Gillette describe it as an immature masculine energy that is "hostile and deprecating of all the real effort, all the rights, all the beauty of others." The Trickster has in common with the High Chair Tyrant the desire to avoid doing anything himself. He uses cunning to avoid earning anything honestly. In the psychology literature this type is described as passive-aggressive.

When the Precocious Child is not connected to the Divine Child, which allows for self-worth, the Trickster will become the guiding force for the individual. This will bring problems in the areas of authority and responsibility. To circumvent this immature behavior, the Precocious Child must seek out and honor the Divine Child in himself. The energy of the Precocious Child, Moore and Gillette note, is the energy of envy, and the envy comes from the Trickster being out of touch with his own creativity. To escape this destructive envy, the Trickster must unleash his creativity by connecting with the Divine Child. It is practically obligatory for the Trickster to find and nurture the Divine Child in himself. By realizing his own specialness and his own beauty, the Trickster can gradually modify his treatment of others.

The other shadow form of the Precocious Child is the Dummy. The Dummy lacks a lust for life and seems to withdraw from life. As the appellation suggests, the Dummy may simply be trying to fool people. He may deliberately wear the dunce cap to conceal how much he knows. There is an element of conceit and grandiosity ("I'm too important to have anything to do with you") in his character. In this way the Dummy is also a Trickster.

The Oedipal Child

The archetype of the Oedipal Child represents inadequate masculine nurturing from adult, mature men. This archetype, according to Moore and Gillette, can be found to some degree in all of the Boy archetypes. Even the boy profoundly lacking in beneficial male nurturing may, however, still be able to experience and express the positive qualities of the archetype.

The characteristics of the Oedipal Child are passion, a sense of wonder, and a deep appreciation for connectedness—with himself, with others, and with his environment. Unlike the Precocious Child, who is also curious about people, the Oedipal Child is a warm and affectionate type. A predominant aspect of the Oedipal Child is his deep sense of connectedness to the Mother, and through the Mother archetype, with the origins of spirituality. The Oedipal Child's appreciation for the oneness of all things is a rewriting, on a cosmic scale, of his desire for the ideal Mother—"the infinitely nurturing, infinitely good, infinitely beautiful Mother."

The shadow forms of the Oedipal Child are typed as the Mama's Boy and the Dreamer. The Mama's Boy longs for union with the goddess (Mother). This longing is expressed in the actions of the individual who runs from woman to woman, wanting to experience them all but satisfied with none. In human love he is constantly searching for the immortal Goddess, and is bound to be disappointed. We recognize this type in the Don Juans of the world. The Mama's Boy will remain dissatisfied in all branches of life because his ultimate yearning, to experience the oneness of all things, suffocates under the weight of his inflated ego.

The Dreamer, on the other hand, takes flight from human relationships in his dreams. The Dreamer lives under a spell, relating by preference to the world of imagination within himself. He has few strong relationships with other people and may appear disinterested.

The Hero

The archetype of the hero represents the most advanced form of the Boy psychology. In this archetype the masculine energies of the boy are most productively used. Yet it is still an immature stage, even if the best an adolescent boy can achieve, and if it continues into adulthood it can cause problems. The adult man who remains a Hero is blocked from reaching full maturity.

The shadow forms of the Hero are the Grandstander Bully and the Coward. The Grandstander Bully asserts himself to be superior to all around him. He inflates himself to a status that is almost godlike, for he acknowledges no limits. He is a child who refuses to see his own mortality.

The Coward refuses to fight for anything. He is repeatedly "beaten up" (or down), and defeated. But when pushed to his limits he, too, has the hidden power of the Bully, which he will use to its full capacity.

According to Moore and Gillette, the presence of the Hero in the male psyche allows the individual to break out of childhood into adulthood. The authors put it this way:

> The Hero energies call upon the boy's masculine reserves, which will be refined as he matures, in order to establish his

independence and his competence, for him to be able to experience his own budding abilities, to "push the outside of the envelope" and test himself against the difficult, even the hostile, forces of the world. The Hero enables him to establish a beachhead against the overwhelming power of the unconscious (much of which, for men at least, is experienced as feminine, the Mother). The Hero enables the boy to begin to assert himself and define himself as distinct from all others, so that ultimately, as a distinct being, he can relate to them fully and creatively.

It is the maturation of the Hero that takes us to the threshold of manhood.

These four archetypes allow us to inventory our own psyches. Each Boy archetype exists in all of us to a greater or lesser degree. These archetypes assert their influence whether we are aware of them or not. By learning about the archetypes, which is part of taking responsibility for ourselves, we can determine where we stand in relation to each of them. The growth process often involves wavering back and forth between the shadow forms until we make a commitment to the positive pole of the archetype and begin to work toward realizing the positive form. This is the first step in the growth from immaturity to maturity. If we do not acknowledge this process, we stay stuck in the shadow forms of the archetypes. If this situation carries over into adulthood, it will express itself in the shadow aspect of the corresponding archetype in the adult psychology, which is built on the childhood psychology. Without the first foundation in place, the second foundation cannot be erected. This prevents us from accessing appropriately the mature aspects of the adult archetypes.

The next step in maturing the male psyche is to move into the archetypal stages of the Man psychology. These archetypes, if one matures fully, come into being as each of the Boy archetypes matures. If maturation of the Boy psychology is stunted, if we remain stuck in one of the shadow aspects of the archetypes, the maturation of the Man psychology will also suffer.

MAN PSYCHOLOGY

King

The King is the most important archetype of the Man psychology; it is also directly tied in to the other three archetypes. The King archetype provides two invaluable functions. One is organization, and the other is fertility and blessing.

In his organizing function the King exhibits order and reason. These qualities allow integration of all the different parts of the male psyche. The King imposes thoughtful order on chaotic emotions and behaviors. He protects our sense of being and defends the certainty of the masculine identity.

The King archetype is concerned with maintenance—with order, calm, and stability—but it is also concerned with sustenance. The King manifests kindly nurturance. Through his ability to center others, the King mediates vitality and creativity. He sees without judging the weaknesses and talents in others, promotes them and honors them. He guides others to achieve the best they can. Remarkably, the King is not envious, for he knows his own worth.

The shadow forms of the King archetype express themselves as either the Tyrant or the Weakling. The Tyrant is similar to the High Chair Tyrant in his thoughts and actions. The Tyrant attacks good things in others, tearing down, never building up. He lacks the essential self-worth and potency of the true King that are requisite to maintaining calm and promoting growth. The Tyrant hates beauty, innocence, talent, and life energy. He exploits others and pursues his own self-interest mercilessly. This is a very harmful shadow figure and one that is driven by fear and the knowledge of personal weakness.

The Weakling King, the other shadow side, is always afraid. He also lacks centeredness and inner security. He acts for himself alone.

To access the King's energy appropriately, we must disengage our individual egos from it. The Shadow King manifests when our egos are directly involved with the archetype's energy. As with all of the archetypes, the ego structure provides the major control mechanism by which the individual ego uses well or uses poorly the energy of the archetype.

Warrior

The Warrior energy in man is the driving force that allows us to perform our duties. The Warrior is aggressive and alert. He has legitimate phallic power. "The Warrior energy is concerned with skill, power, and accuracy, and with control, both inner and outer, psychological and physical."

The Warrior is always subject to a higher cause than himself. He is in service to, ideally, the King. As is true for all the archetypes, the Warrior must access the other archetypes in order to be effective in his role. The Warrior needs the Magician to master his craft, and the Lover to help him remain connected with humanity. Without these links to the other archetypes the Warrior will fall victim to the shadow forms of the archetype, which manifest as the Sadist and the Masochist.

The Sadist lacks control over his feelings. Cruelty flows from him. He becomes an avenger who acts from fear instead of inner strength. His vision is blurred, his senses are numb.

The Masochist cannot defend himself. He is a coward. He resentfully lets life and other people overpower him until he finally explodes into the shadow form of the Sadist. These bipolar shadow forms of the Warrior feed on each other viciously.

Both shadow forms of the Warrior carry into adulthood the adolescent insecurity and desperation of the Boy psychology. The Shadow Warrior has a complicated relationship to the feminine, which he regards as inordinately powerful and a threat to his own phallic power. His fear of the feminine—for the feminine questions his essence—may be expressed in acts of brutality. Because the feminine summates our relational nature, the Shadow Warrior, to escape the feminine, cuts off other people and privileges his own solitary strength.

There are many good aspects to the Warrior: courage, energy, strength, conviction, perseverance, loyalty. In the ideal Warrior, these sustaining qualities are all turned outward and put in the service of some greater good. Accessing the other archetypes will help the Warrior shine in his domain of masculine energy.

Magician

The archetype of the magician represents knowledge. He has the ability to think things through and understand them. The energies of the Magician are expressed in two ways. One way, the Magician acquires knowledge; he may show special mastery of technology. In the second way the Magician is able to draw on rituals to fulfill his functions. As a "ritual elder," the Magician guides the processes of transformation, in whatever form these transformations take.

The human Magician learns through training and initiation, and in turn trains and initiates others. His area of expertise is the "secret and hidden knowledge of all kinds. [. . .] All knowledge that takes special training to acquire is the province of the Magician energy."

In ancient times, the Magicians were the Gnostics. As Moore and Gillette write,

> Gnosis was the Greek word for "knowing" on a deep psychological or spiritual level. The Gnostics were knowers of the inner depths of the human psyche and the hidden dynamics of the universe. They were really proto-depth psychologists. They taught their initiates how to discover their own motives and drives, how to thread their way through the treacherous darkness of human delusions, and how, finally, to reach oneness with the Center that lies deep within.

The Magician archetype that inhabits our psyches provides the energy we need in order to progress in our personal transformation. Accessing the Magician helps us access hidden knowledge. The Magician speaks best in a sacred place dedicated to this personal transformation. The Magician observes our lives and directs us safely on our path.

The shadow forms of the Magician are the Manipulator and the Innocent One. Instead of directing others with information, the Manipulator does just the opposite: he withholds information that is needed for growth. He does this in order to control others and retain power for himself. The Innocent One wants the Magician's powers but not his responsibilities. He learns just enough to maintain some degree of control over others. He has no interest in learning and teaching the ways of the Magician. He holds others in check along with himself.

Lover

The archetype of the Lover experiences connectedness with all things. Boundaries are nonexistent for the Lover. He is fundamentally sensual in all things. Poets, artists, and musicians access the Lover's energies when they create. The archetype of the Lover allows one to experience fully both the joy and the pain of life.

The Lover with a strong ego structure seems to enjoy the best in life. He is empathic, compassionate, and romantic about his life and his achievements. He is enthusiastic and energetic. Properly accessed, the Lover in us can provide a sense of meaning in life. The Lover longs for a better world for himself and others.

The shadow forms of the Lover are the Addicted Lover and the Impotent Lover. These forms generally suffer from a weak ego structure. The Addicted Lover is one who has no limits to his sensuality. He becomes overwhelmed by his feelings and is easily carried away by whatever feeling possesses him at the moment. His actions become destructive to himself and others around him. Because he has no boundaries, he is wide open to any incoming impressions. He is forever restless.

The Impotent Lover has lost his lust for life. He becomes withdrawn and depressed. His world seems mundane, and he cannot assert himself sufficiently to effect a change.

The Lover must be connected to all of the other archetypes in order to function properly. He needs them as much as they need him. A balance among all the archetypes brings a balance to the individual and the individual's relations with the world.

The archetypes of the Boy psychology and the Man psychology are present in the life of an adult individual in all their forms, both their ideal forms and their shadow forms. We may be accessing the mature King one minute and the High Chair Tyrant in the next minute. When we integrate the archetypes in their positive forms into our lives, we transform not only ourselves but those around us. If someone enters a room full of stringed instruments and plucks a C string, the C chords of all the instruments will also vibrate through their harmonic ranges. So it is with life. When one person begins to vibrate at a higher level, those around him will also start to vibrate.

The archetypal structure devised by Moore and Gillette gave me a framework I could use to sort out the different levels of my psyche. This process also required the use of active imagination. With the knowledge I gained about myself, I was able to identify the way each archetype manifested in my life, and then to re-integrate the shadow forms. Once I discovered this system, the results of my therapy sessions progressed tenfold.

THE EGO

The condition of the ego largely influences how we access and use psychic archetypes. For it is the ego structure of the individual that is capable of integrating the bipolar shadows of the archetypes and transforming them upwards. If the ego structure is weak, this transformation cannot take place, and we will be consigned to live in the shadow forms. The power of the archetypes can overwhelm a weak ego and nullify what the ego wants to accomplish.

Moore and Gillette envision the ego as positioned somewhat "above" the spatiotemporal dimension, in the domain of the spirit. From this position the ego can fix its attention on the ideal, transcendent forms of the archetypes. The archetypes themselves are expressed in time and space, and the ego is the chief agent of this expression. If the ego itself is constrained to work in the spatiotemporal dimension, only the polar shadow forms of the archetypes will be available to the individual. In this respect we can think of the ego as providing a buffer between the conscious and the unconscious. If the ego is deficient or corrupt, the messages transferred between the conscious and the unconscious will be degraded.

The ultimate function of the ego in respect to archetypes is to transform and channel the energy of the archetypes into a form usable by the individual. A strong, consolidated ego is able to balance the energies of the ego structure against the energies of the archetypes. The ego structure functions as the fulcrum of an axis, the two ends of which are occupied by the individual ego and the archetypes. We can also think of the ego structure as a transformer that powers down and controls the flow of energy from the archetypes into the individual's ego. In the words of Moore and

Gillette, "Ego structure is the psychological equivalent of the shielding and transforming systems noted in the ancient rituals and in modern technology. . . . This concentrates the energy of the archetype within the archetypal structure, and protects the rest of the psyche from being flooded by its expansive Libido."

The idea of the ego structure as a transformer that "powers down" the energy of the archetype and makes it available to the individual became an important source of information for me. I tend to live predominantly in the archetype of the Magician, the Man psychology counterpart to the Precocious Boy that wants to know everything. You remember that during my third manic episode I experienced myself as a "wizard's wizard." I now wonder whether the inability of my ego structure to contain and "power down" the energy of the Magician archetype allowed my psyche to be drawn wholly into the archetypal world of the Magician. My weak ego might have been deluged by the power of the archetype, leading to further weakening of the ego and a deterioration of my psychological structure severe enough to warrant hospitalization. All of the pieces seem to fit this view.

Depression

Manic-depression has three distinct modes of expression. In one, the individual swings from one extreme to the other, and thus is truly bipolar. In a second condition, known as the manic-depressive-depressive state, the individual experiences only the depressive aspects and no mania. In the third type the individual experiences only the mania and thus is manic-depressive-manic. This last category encompasses only five percent of the people with this "illness."

I fall into the third category. Although I do get depressed, it is not the totally debilitating depression that others seem to experience. From my own experience, then, I have little to offer on this subject, for my experience has not allowed me a glimpse into the depths of depression. But early in my investigations of manic-depression, before I knew which type I was, I came across some interesting thoughts which suggest that depression, like mania, has a positive side. Depression can be used to clear out accumulated debris and restructure our psyche, if we know how to use it.

In Care of the Soul, Thomas Moore refers depression, or melancholy, as it was called in the past, to the Roman god Saturn. Saturn is usually characterized as cold and distant, and it was for these characteristics that the ancient astronomers so named the planet in our solar system. But, as Moore points out, Saturn is also the god of wisdom and reflection. Depression can then be understood as an opportunity to reflect on and evaluate our lives. It is a time of inner growth. Instead of trying to escape the dark moods, we can allow them into our lives, honoring their unusual qualities and contributions.

Moore writes,

> In recommending some positive effects in saturnine moods, I
> don't want to overlook the terrible pain they bring. Nor is it
> only minor forms of melancholy that offer gifts to the soul;
> long, deep bouts of acute depression can also clear out and
> restructure the tenets by which life has been lived.

If we deny depression, then we are denying part of who
we are, part of our soul. And in denying it we empower it
all the more because it cannot be destroyed. It will respond
as any other repressed emotion: it will seep out in ways we
may or may not be conscious of.

In the book, *Touched With Fire,* Kay Redfield Jamison
writes that melancholy, a mild form of depression, can actually create a balance in our lives by adding periods of quiet
reflection to what we do in moments of high enthusiasm:

> Melancholy . . . tends to force a slower pace, cools the ardor,
> and puts into perspective the thoughts, observations, and feel-
> ings generated during more enthusiastic moments. Mild
> depression can act as a ballast; it can also serve a more critical
> role for work produced in more fevered states. Depression
> prunes and sculpts; it also ruminates and ponders and, ulti-
> mately, subdues and focuses thought. It allows restructuring,
> at a detailed level, of the more expansive patterns woven dur-
> ing hypomania.

Melancholy as a tool for sculpting and pondering on the
works generated by high enthusiasm echoes an important
concept in Christian Hermeticism, namely, that the pure
mystical experience must be followed by reflection. This is

expressed in the High Priestess, the second card of the tarot. After the active principle is experienced the passive principle must follow so that the unknown may be made known to the conscious mind. If we allow depression to serve knowledge, then we can access it as a tool for personal growth. In Jungian terms, depression is "negative inflation," the other face of positive inflation or megalomania. In the state of negative inflation, the individual is convinced he will never be fulfilled, thus confirming his own inferiority. Jung said that positive inflation and negation inflation go hand in hand; you can never have one without the other. Understood this way, depression becomes just another hurdle to be cleared in the process of self-transformation.

Depression also offers a more sobering perspective on life. According to Kay Jamison, depression forces us to look at death. It forces us to consider "the fleeting nature of life," and "the finite role played by man in the history of the universe." Moore returns this idea to the land of the living by suggesting that depression creates a space for mystery in our neatly tied and packaged lives. Just as the ancient astronomers saw Saturn as the outermost planet, remote, unfathomable, and mysterious, so the saturnalia of depression "makes holes in our theories and assumptions, but even this painful process can be honored as a necessary and valuable source of healing."

In today's society of the quick fix, the individual who seeks help from modern medicine very often does not get the understanding that he or she is seeking. Instead, the individual gets an antidepressant. This all comes back to the responsibility of the individual for his or her own life. This is a responsibility that every individual must accept and not just turn over to others.

Psychosynthesis

I have been hospitalized in three separate institutions that handle individuals who experience psychological states different from the accepted "normal" state. Not once was it ever mentioned or suggested that my experience could be anything other than an illness. When I found the courage to raise the possibility that I might be going through a psychic transformation, rather than experiencing an illness, I was told I was in denial, and that that was part of the illness. It took a long time for me to believe fully in myself, without transferring into my mind the uneducated thoughts of other people.

In developing the connection between mania and "awakening," I was greatly aided by a book by Roberto Assagioli titled *Psychosynthesis.* Although this book was first published in the United States in 1965, I did not come across it until very recently. Whether I might have understood it back in 1980, when I started my investigation into mania, is anyone's guess. What I find incredible is that this book has been around for some time, but its content has not been assimilated into modern American psychoanalytical practice. It is all the more surprising because Assagioli was a leader of the Italian school of psychoanalytic theory and a colleague of Jung, Freud, and Maslow.

Assagioli's concept of psychosynthesis involves a restructuring of the personality through increasing knowledge of the elements of one's personality. It is a form of ego development that creates room for the individual yearning for a higher state. In developing a functional harmonious relationship with himself and with others, the individual must pass through four distinct stages. These are:

1. Thorough knowledge of one's personality
2. Control of its various elements

3. Realization of one's true self—the discovery or creation of a unifying center
4. Psychosynthesis: the formation or reconstruction of the personality around the new center

In the first step, acquiring knowledge of one's personality, we explore the various areas of our minds, both the conscious and the unconscious aspects. In the course of this in-depth survey of ourselves we will be able to discover

unknown abilities, our true vocations, our higher potentialities which seek to express themselves, but which we often repel and repress through lack of understanding, through prejudice or fear. We shall also discover the immense reserve of undifferentiated psychic energy latent in every one of us; that is, the plastic part of our unconscious which lies at our disposal, empowering us with unlimited capacity to learn and to create.

Once this investigation into our personality is complete and we become aware of the various elements of our personality, we can begin to learn how to control them instead of being controlled by them. This is done by disidentification. Disidentification occurs when we are able to see these elements as a manifestation of our energy and not who we really are. For example, if I feel angry, I can distance myself from my emotion by saying, "the feeling of anger is coming over me." This allows me to separate myself from the emotion, which does not suppress the energy but gives me the opportunity to redirect the energy.

The third stage in psychosynthesis is the realization of one's true self. Ideally, this stage should come about naturally in the growth of the individual. In the realization of the true self, the individual understands that there is within his grasp something higher than what he has experienced so far in life. The individual becomes aware of an ideal, a higher self, to strive for. This higher self ideally should be felt by the individual, but it may also be projected onto someone else who exemplifies the ideal. The guru in an ashram often serves the function of being the person onto whom this projection is made. The guru thus becomes the symbol for the individual's higher self. The ideal self becomes the new center for organizing the personality around.

In the final stage, a new personality is synthesized to complement the new center of the higher self. Synthesis of the personality entails the use of energies that have been released through the preceding three stages. During the restructuring of the personality, any deficiencies can be corrected, and the energies released are organized so that they can exist together as a complete unit.

It is evident that psychosynthesis applies first to the maturation of the personality, and then to building a bridge that connects the mature individual with the higher self. Assagioli speculated that there is a divine order of things that is always directing creation toward a harmony that will eventually result in the Supreme Synthesis.

SPIRITUAL PSYCHOSYNTHESIS

I mentioned earlier in this book that a spiritual experience can occur without the self having fully matured. This is also a point that Assagioli made. In discussing spiritual development, Assagioli said,

Man's spiritual development is a long and arduous journey, an adventure through strange lands full of surprises, difficulties and even dangers. It involves a drastic transmutation of the "normal" elements of the personality, an awakening of potentialities hitherto dormant, a raising of consciousness to new realms, and a functioning along a new inner dimension.

The change from the lower self to the higher self, in Assagioli's view, is marked by the individual going through confused states that encompass the emotional and mental levels of his being. The resulting disturbances may appear no different from symptoms due to other, quite different causes. The clinical therapist, Assagioli warned, may confuse the symptoms of personal growth with symptoms of other problems, but in reality they have a different significance and need different treatment.

Assagioli outlined some of the disturbances that can occur as the self awakens to its true nature and begins reconstructing the personality. These are:

1. Crises preceding the spiritual awakening
2. Crises caused by the spiritual awakening
3. Reactions to the spiritual awakening
4. Phases of the process of transmutation

I will explain each of these four stages in turn, for they expose the process of psychosynthesis.

Crises Preceding the Spiritual Awakening

The average person goes through life in the way that society has structured it. He goes to school to get the necessary tools so that he can function in society. He follows his own ideas of what life has to offer him and seeks to fulfill his ambitions. He takes on the responsibilities of marriage and the social duties that pertain to his position in society. He may become involved in a particular religion that he feels fulfills his spiritual needs. His life goes on smoothly.

At some point, however, the individual begins to feel incomplete. Many have referred to this period as a midlife crisis. Things that seemed important lose their value. A sense of uncertainty pervades the individual's thoughts.

People may reach this stage without any understanding of what is happening to them. They may regard unusual yearnings as "abnormal fancies and vagaries," per Assagioli. Fearful of what these changes might portend, and particularly afraid of the possibility of mental illness, they may undertake "frantic efforts to re-attach themselves to the 'reality of ordinary life that seems to be slipping away from them.' "

The psychological disturbances preceding a spiritual awakening may take the form of depression and may lead to thoughts of self-destruction. This stage is accompanied by a high level of stress whose source cannot be determined. Assagioli said that these disturbances are best understood as signs that the personality is growing. New aspirations and tendencies, particularly those of a moral, religious, or spiritual character, can produce the conflicts seen by others as manifestations of illness.

Crises Caused by the Spiritual Awakening

When the opening of the lower self to the higher self (or Self) is experienced in the normal growth of consciousness, the individual is released from the confusion that he has been experiencing throughout the growth process. If, however, the individual is not firmly grounded in the various aspects of his personality, another situation develops:

> [I]n some cases, not infrequent, the personality is inadequate in one or more aspects and therefore unable to rightly assimilate the inflow of light and strength. This happens, for instance, when the intellect is not balanced, or the emotions and the imagination are uncontrolled; when the nervous system is too sensitive; or when the inrush of spiritual energy is overwhelming in its suddenness and intensity.

An incapacity of the mind to stand the illumination, or a tendency to egotism or conceit, may cause the experience to be wrongly interpreted, and there results, so to speak, a "confusion of levels." The distinction between absolute and relative truths, between the Self and the "I", is blurred and the inflowing spiritual energies may have the unfortunate effect of feeding and inflating the personal ego.

In mania, this is precisely what occurs. The individual has not developed his personality, which is still in a state of immaturity. It cannot possibly handle the extraordinary power of the spiritual awakening and becomes its victim. The situation remains at this plateau until such time as the individual sufficiently develops his personality to be able to handle the energies of the spiritual aspect of his being. A person experiencing mania tends to make the fatal error of attributing the qualities of the higher Self to the ego self. Assagioli saw this tendency to confuse the two selves as a manifestation of "confusion between an absolute and a relative truth, between the metaphysical and the empirical levels of reality; in religious terms, between God and the 'soul.'"

Reactions to the Spiritual Awakening

The state that accompanies a spiritual awakening brings with it an understanding of the meaning of life. The individual experiences the oneness in all things and a sense of love and beauty in the world. This experience is only temporary and in time will recede from consciousness, leaving only the memory and a fading image of the event. With its passing, it leaves an individual who is now living between two seemingly separate worlds. The deficiencies of the personality may now be starkly revealed and ruthlessly employed. Assagioli wrote,

> The personal ego re-awakens and asserts itself with renewed force. All the rocks and rubbish, which had been covered and concealed at high tide, emerge again. The man, whose moral conscience has now become more intense, judges with greater severity and condemns his personality with a new vehemence; he is apt to harbor the false belief of having fallen lower than he was before. Sometimes it happens that the lower propensities and drives, hitherto lying dormant in the conscious, are vitalized by the inrush of higher energy, or stirred into a fury of opposition by the consecration of the awakening man—a fact which constitutes a challenge and a menace to their uncontrolled expression.

To recapitulate the process from the beginning, the individual who is "initiated" into the higher aspect of his being through the natural growth of consciousness is given a taste of the harmonious world of the spirit. It is a world that he is part of and can attain. But as this initial exposure recedes, the individual comes back to the reality of the lower self. This return to reality produces uncertainty and confusion if it is not understood properly:

> Sometimes the reaction presents a more pathological aspect and produces a state of depression and even despair, with suicidal impulses. This state bears a close resemblance to psychotic depression or "melancholia" which is characterized by an acute sense of unworthiness, a systematic self-depreciation, and self-accusation; the impression of going through hell, which might become so vivid as to produce the delusion that one is irretrievably damned; a keen and painful sense of intellectual incompetence; a loss of will power and self-control, indecision and an incapacity and distaste for action.

This passage speaks for itself. Assagioli used the word "sometimes" in regard to this process, which suggests that it does not happen in every case. The other point I want to draw attention to is that this state of depression closely resembles psychotic depression. Who is fit to make the determining judgment of the experience? In medical institutions today, in my experience, no consideration is given to the possibility of a spiritual awakening. When this is the case, there can be only one diagnosis.

Assagioli was a practicing psychoanalyst, and one of his concerns was the proper diagnosis and treatment of people in the grip of a spiritual crisis. Treatment, he thought, should consist in helping the individual understand the true nature of the experience and then use it in a fruitful way. A guiding hand during the fall after the initial awakening will greatly help the individual get through this phase of growth:

> It should be made clear to him that the exalted state he has experienced could not, by its very nature, last forever and that reaction was inevitable. It is as though he has made a superb flight to the sunlight mountain top, realized its glory and the beauty of the panorama spread below, but has been brought back reluctantly to his starting point with the rueful recognition that the steep path leading to the heights must be climbed step by step. The recognition that this descent or "fall" is a natural happening affords emotional and mental relief and encourages the subject to undertake the arduous task confronting him on the path to self-realization.

Phases of the Process of Transmutation

Once the "initiation" has taken place, the individual finds himself in an uncomfortable place. In the words of Matthew Arnold, the individual is

> Wandering between two worlds
> One dead, The other powerless to be born.

In most cases the individual must endure and pass through several transitional phases while at the same time carrying out the quotidian responsibilities he has shouldered in the world. His family and his work must be taken care of, which adds to the strain of the process he is undergoing. The reorganization of the personality is not a smooth road. It is full of turns and detours. It is a process that cannot be speeded up or forced to a conclusion by the efforts of the individual to "get through it." Rather, the process involves the slow, harmonious integration of all aspects of the personality and the redirection of energies. Assagioli summarized the process of psychosynthesis this way:

> The basic purpose of psychosynthesis is to release or, let us say, help release, the energies of the self. Prior to this the purpose is to help integrate, to synthesize, the individual around the personal self, and then later to effect the synthesis between the personal ego and the Self.

In starting to restructure his personality, the individual must understand that the energies being released must be channeled in a constructive way. If these energies are left to themselves, they may cause havoc. If, however, these energies are accessed properly, the path to full integration with the higher self becomes less of a struggle and more like an adventure. Life becomes a new and wondrous gift to experience.

◉

Assagioli's work helps us understand that there is, in human development, a time for spiritual growth, and that spiritual growth tends to occur in definite stages. Assagioli and his peers, Maslow and Jung, all agreed that spirituality is the central fact of man's highest functioning. Although I am sure that these ideas are presently used by some of the more enlightened individuals in science, to my mind, mainstream psychology today has taken an ungodly path in its neglect of human spiritual growth. But the saving grace is that all paths eventually lead to the truth, so in time I am sure the situation will change.

The Dawn of the Soul

All the times that I've cried

keeping all the things I knew inside

it's hard, but it's harder to ignore it.

If they were right I'd agree

but it's them they know not me

now there's a way and I know. . . .

CAT STEVENS
"FATHER AND SON"

I began this work with a quotation from Teilhard de Chardin: "We are not human beings having a spiritual experience, we are spiritual beings having a human experience." I would now like to advance this truth in one important way. I believe we are both. I believe we are human beings having a spiritual experience and spiritual beings having a human experience.

The idea that human beings are part of the universal whole has been noted and remarked on down through time. Humans have assigned this oneness different names: God, Tao, Brahman, Allah, energy. It is the same principle interpreted by different minds at different times.

Years ago, when I began trying to understand my experiences with mania, I also tried to stay away from the religious aspects of what I was finding out. I had been raised in Roman Catholicism, with its ferocious emphasis on guilt and sin, and I did not want to get tangled up in any more constrictions. But as my investigations continued, I slowly shifted into the world of spirituality. This proved to be an inevitable step, for ego psychology and studies of the mind seem to converge at the point where spiritual growth enters the picture. Although spirituality and religion are woven together, they are also vastly different. In this way I was able to use the ideas of spirituality from different religions without having to practice those religions or share in all their beliefs.

I will not try to lead anyone to or away from what they believe or what religion they follow. Those are personal choices. I know only what I have found out for myself. And what I have found out is that the illness known as mania is not an illness at all. In fact, it is the most precious gift of all.

One of the most annoying problems I have run into during my search is that the word mania suggests only one thing, illness. I will now redefine it so that in the future, others will have a choice.

Mania is the genesis of awareness to the dawning of the soul.

This definition may not be complete in its present form, but for now I find that it satisfies the vacancy that exists.

I would now like to review the investigations I conducted and the different experiences I underwent to develop this understanding of mania. In the beginning of this book I related my first experience with mania, just as it unfolded. A sudden shift in consciousness took me to the heights of the heavens, then sent me crashing back to earth. After I was picked up and dusted off, I continued on with my life, now carrying the label of mental illness. I turned over the responsibility for my experience to the medical profession, followed its advice, and tried not to think too much about what had happened.

My journey toward self-knowledge truly began when I decided to take responsibility for myself and my experiences. I started at the bottom, with the known physical world, my diet. I began eating only foods that were really foods and not tainted by the needs of commerce. This exploration in the physical plane expanded to include exercise, sleep, and meditation; and from meditation I stepped into the world of the mind.

With my second episode, which did not progress beyond hypomania, I became intrigued by the powers of the mind. I set as the only goal of my life "to fully understand the workings of my mind." To this end I began looking for any information that would allow me a greater understanding of the functioning of the mind. During this search I came across the work of Thomas Jay Hudson, which supplied me with a structural foundation that allowed me to start my quest.

In reading about the mind, I soon found myself faced with a dilemma. I had come to the crossroads of the mental realm and the spiritual realm. All the weighty considerations of mind and soul boiled down to two questions: Was I god? And if so, how was I to become what I was? The choice was made: I wanted to be god!

Mania struck again, when it was not expected, and I entered a world of fairies and wizards. My imagination ran away with my reason, and the result was a ticket to the hospital good for two weeks.

After this episode I began looking closely into the powers of the imagination and the relationship of imagination to concentration and will. To explore some of these ideas in solitude, I sent myself on a walk through the woods and stepped into Christian Hermeticism. This journey, both physical and spiritual, helped me link together the psychological and spiritual aspects of man.

A fourth time I would face the dragon and a third time fall victim to its powers. But this experience set the stage for the immature parts of me to die off and maturity to take root. A signal part of this maturity was coming to the realization that I could not successfully continue the process of growth alone. I gathered up enough courage to look for a therapist, and was extremely fortunate to find Natalie Rogers. At about the same time that I started therapy I began reading about myths and archetypes, searching for missing pieces. Personal therapy and myths intersected in ego psychology, and so I began an in-depth study of my psychological makeup and temperament.

Subsequently I found more information on imagination and became immersed in the study of archetypes, which would become tools for understanding my psyche. Finally, I came back to the work of Roberto Assagioli on psychosynthesis and was able to learn more about the process of spiritual awakening and the steps involved in that process.

This summary gives a road map of my experience and brings us up to the present, but like all road maps it obscures the land forms that we traverse and the felt residue they leave in our hearts and minds. The following section places this road map in the context of maturing as a spiritual being.

AWAKENING, NOT ILLNESS

Human development, when properly achieved, integrates our ego self with our higher Self. These are terms from modern psychology, and they are almost infinitely replaceable by other words, depending on the system of thought you are using on your personal journey. The early years of development, which I would say are loosely from birth to age thirty-five years, are the time during which the individual learns about his or her physical and mental being. The individual must mature from the child to the adult in the early years of life. Once he reaches physical and mental maturity he can be "born again" as a spiritual being. And just as the growth from immaturity to maturity completes the self, so spiritual growth advances the self to the Self. The ultimate goal is to bring together self with Self in total awareness.

According to the 1988 *Encyclopedia Americana,* volume 18, the major occurrences of manic-depression happen in the third and fourth decades of life. In other words, manic-depression makes its appearance at about the time the individual is completing physical and mental growth and readying him- or herself for spiritual growth. The temporal connection seems obvious, but we as a race are not smart. We remain caught in our ignorance, fears, and antiquated thoughts. In the words of Albert Einstein, "Two things are infinite: the universe and human stupidity."

According to the *Academic American Encyclopedia,* ninety percent of people affected by manic-depression recover without treatment. If manic-depression represents a rapid plunge into spiritual growth, as I believe, and not an "illness," then medical treatment isn't going to "cure" it anyway. The soul is restless and ready to move ahead. It is time that we began thinking of manic-depression as an initiation into a spirituality that all humans are capable of achieving in some fashion. It is a reminder that we are not only humans having a spiritual experience, we are also spiritual beings having a human experience.

It is evident that we have lost our connection to who and what we are. Earlier I quoted the Russian philosopher Ouspensky as saying that the meaning of life consists in knowledge. But I found myself asking, "Knowledge of what?" The answer came readily, for in virtually every spiritual discipline, the end of knowledge is self-knowledge: knowledge of who you are in the trinity of mind, body, and spirit; knowledge that can only be found by one who seeks, knocks, asks, and listens. The path to self-knowledge is a personal path that can only be taken by the individual. You may be assisted by others, but you and you alone must bring yourself with your questions. And you must be guided by your ignorance, for your ignorance will be your teacher. You must become as open as a child.

Our world is not structured for personal growth toward a union of the self with the Self. At times, in fact, it seems violently opposed to personal growth. But the path to this goal has never changed, and it becomes easy to follow once you know what you don't know.

Life is a constant process of growth toward a union with the higher Self. In this respect we are all, in one way or another, yogis. Whether or not we consciously choose to take this path will determine the pace of our growth.

In Chapter 12 I mentioned the four branches of yoga—Bhakti, Karma, Raja, and Jnana. It is interesting that these four branches resemble the four archetypes that Robert Moore and Douglas Gillette outlined for the modern masculine psyche. Bhakti yoga is the path of devotion, which falls into the Lover archetype. Karma yoga teaches us to act selflessly, without thought of gain or reward—the realm of the King. Raja yoga is the science of physical and mental control—the characteristics of the Warrior. And finally, Jnana yoga, which uses the mind to inquire into its own nature, is the way of the Magician. These four paths of yoga and the four modern archetypes of the masculine psyche also align well with the four temperaments identified by David Keirsey and Marilyn Bates, which are the Apollonian, Dionysian, Epimethean, and Promethean temperaments.

As it turns out, I happen to live in the realm of the Magician. As I began searching for the meaning and cause of my experience, I used my mind to inquire into its own nature—the path of a Jnana yogi, the correlative of the Magician. This process has taken nearly thirteen years, or enough time to complete high school, college, and most of a Ph.D. program. The only difference was there was only one subject, myself.

My course has not been easy, and I did not advance on all levels simultaneously. Nevertheless, I did go through certain stages in a fairly well-defined order that has been identified by many analysts and spiritual thinkers as the usual stages in the development of spirituality. Each stage prepared me for the next stage and opened up connections I could not have made otherwise.

I started on the simplest physical level, by learning how food affects my body and mind. It took almost ten years before I found someone who knew how food works. With this information, I was able to move to the mind. I looked for information on how the conscious mind and the unconscious mind function, especially in respect to their different reasoning powers. I then sought out information on human spirituality. The search had to progress in this order because each plane is built on the one below it, although all are intertwined.

After learning about the structure of human growth, I had to begin the long arduous journey to the mature ego self, and then toward an integration with the Self. This is the first stage in what Assagioli called personal psychosynthesis. This stage entails

> helping the patient to reach the normal state of the average man or woman by means of the elimination of repressions and inhibitions, of fears and childish dependence; to find his way out of his self-centeredness, his emotionally distorted outlook, into an objective, sane and rational consideration of normal life, into a recognition of its duties and obligations, and a right appreciation of other individuals.

The second stage of growth is spiritual psychosynthesis of the individual by means of what Jung called the re-centering of the ego. In this stage the individual becomes aware of the higher aspects of his or her being and begins to understand that changes have to be made for growth to proceed. In the book *Growing Sane,* by James Stallone and Sy Migdal, which I discussed in Chapter 17, the authors explain the psychological disturbances that may accompany spiritual growth, and how these disturbances can be sorted out from disturbances due to other causes.

The first stage, synthesis of the ego, and the second stage, spiritual psychosynthesis, are never entirely separate stages, and this has proved a particular problem for modern therapy to face. The stages overlap, in time and in symptoms, and what is helpful for growth in one stage may be detrimental to growth in the other stage. Roberto Assagioli recognized this problem and stated that a twofold competence is required. The therapist should be a professionally trained psychotherapist and the patient a serious student along the path of self-realization. In my case both of these prerequisites were met.

When I met Natalie Rogers and began therapy, I was stuck in both stages of growth. I was trying to develop personal maturity at the same time that I was trying to develop spiritual maturity. It was difficult at first to sort out the personal confusion from the spiritual confusion. The personal confusion had what Assagioli termed a regressive character, where the individual is not maturing properly. According to Assagioli, this derailment in personal growth can be the result of an emotional attachment to the parents that carries over into adult life inappropriately, or it may be brought on by

emotional shock or bereavement that [the individual] cannot or will not accept, which may lead to reactive depression or other neurotic symptoms. In all these cases we find, as a common characteristic, some conflict or conflicts, between various conscious and unconscious aspects of the personality, or between the personality and its environment.

In my case, it seems to have been the second cause, a reactive depression with subsequent conflict, that stood in the way of personal growth. I would now like to present my case from the viewpoint of Natalie Rogers, who provided the following summary. You will readily see the kinds of conflicts I was embroiled in, and how my personal growth could have remained rooted to the spot until these conflicts were resolved.

For many years Bob had an intensely ambivalent relationship with his one-year-older brother Paul. On the one hand, Bob admired and adored Paul; however, owing to his brother's unrelentingly harsh and abusive behavior, Bob developed a deep hostility and rage that was directed towards his brother. When Paul was eighteen years old he was killed in an automobile accident. Bob experienced an unbearable guilt because of the hatred he had harbored against Paul. In addition, Bob was culturally inhibited about expressing the deep grief that the loss of his brother evoked.

The explosive intensity of these unresolved, unexpressed emotions caused the conflict that catapulted Bob into his first manic episode. It was as if his brain was unable to continue containing and repressing the immensity of these volatile emotions, and so he simply exploded into mania and was finally able to express the rage and grief he was feeling in the form of manic behavior. Subsequently, unexpressed grief and rage emerged in the form of hyperactivity and were the triggers for future manic episodes.

The particular behavior that assisted Bob in masking his grief was the sexual pursuit and conquest of women, one after another. All of these conquests ended with Bob abandoning these women, just as he would have loved to have abandoned his brother as punishment for Paul's abusive behavior.

As the pattern of manic episodes emerged over a fifteen-year period, occurring every three or four years, the original triggers of grief and rage expanded to include other high-intensity emotions. Even a situation of intense joy and self-satisfaction was enough to shift Bob's behavior into a hyperactive state and finally into a complete manic breakdown. This was demonstrated in his last manic episode, which occurred four years ago. At that time Bob believed he had finally found the perfect job. As staff manager for the Omega Institute, a holistic center for individuals that offered courses in alternative healing and New Age philosophies, Bob was in charge of the daily operation and maintenance of the housekeeping department. He quickly mastered the complexity of this new operation, running his department and managing the staff with such skill that, as he said, the self-esteem he experienced was "too much to bear." Not being able to contain the excitement he felt, his shift into hyperactivity was inevitable, as was the manic episode that followed.

It took some time for me to understand the personal issues underlying my conflicted emotional state, and then to begin resolving these conflicts. This was an important moment, for with the resolution of conflict, healing could begin.

HEALING

It wasn't until the summer of 1993 that a major healing occurred. It happened after a therapy session I had had in the morning. I was home getting ready for bed when an intense feeling of grief came over me. As thoughts of my brother filled my mind, tears began to run down my face. The grief seemed to come in waves, slowly at first and then increasing in pace and intensity. I had to sit down because my legs would not hold me. My crying turned into sobs that came from deep within me.

And then it hit me. It felt as if someone was ripping my mind apart. My head started to tingle. Oh God help me, not again, please, not again! As the pain intensified I was consumed by panic. I didn't know what to do. Please! Somebody help me, please! I reached for the phone, but I could not see the numbers through my tears. I had to dial by remembering the pattern of the buttons. I called Natalie Rogers at home, waking her.

—It's happening again—please help me!

—Bob, Bob, where are you?

—I'm home.

—What is happening?

—I don't know—I had thoughts of my brother's death, and then my head felt as if it were being ripped apart. I think I'm going to go manic—please help me!

—Bob, find something that is heavy and pick it up.

—OK, I have a phone book.

—Listen, Bob, you are not going to go manic. What you are feeling is the grief you have never gone through. Before, when you did not go into it you went manic. You have now started to grieve, and by doing this you have kept yourself from going manic. How are you feeling now?

—Alright. I'm tired and hungry.

—Get something to eat, then rest.

This was the beginning of a healing process that took twenty-two years to appear. It was the dividing line between sanity and insanity. Although the process was and is painful at times, the knowledge I have gained carries me through it.

THE JOURNEY OF LIFE

Getting my personal house in order was part of personal psychosynthesis. The conflicts in this stage of growth, as Assagioli noted, are of a regressive character because they are tied in to our lower selves, which pull us backward to a childish, immature state. The confusion that arises during the second stage, or spiritual psychosynthesis, on the other hand, has a "progressive" character because it results from a "call from above . . . the pull of the Self." The conflicts that emerge during spiritual psychosynthesis "are specifically determined by the ensuing maladjustments and conflicts with the 'middle' and 'lower' aspects of personality," Assagioli said.

The path from the self to the Self is the journey of life. We are travelers on this path whether we acknowledge it or not. For myself, I was forced onto the path early in life, and it has taken some years to come to terms with it. But now I have some understanding of what is going on, and it is just a matter of learning what one needs to know.

In the recently published book, *Touched With Fire,* the author, Kay Redfield Jamison, draws the convincing conclusion that many of the world's great artists have been manic-depressives. It has been said many times over that the poets of the day are the mystics of society. A mystic is a person who has had a mystical experience, a direct communication with God. (I have suggested elsewhere in this book how "God" might be interpreted.) It stands to reason, then, that the manic-depressives of society are also our mystics. Actually, they are initiated into the mystical universe whether they like it or not. Whether they will develop into functional mystics lies with the individual. But it seems clear that great poets and artists have occasionally been able to traverse the realms of the mystical and record their experiences, letting the ineffable speak for itself.

Our society does not honor mystics. There is no "place at the table" for them, nowhere for them to lay their heads. Because they stand considerably outside the social structure, there are also no designated teachers. Where do the "initiates" turn to learn what they need to know? They must teach themselves, a monumental task even if they know what they have to learn. But frequently they do not have even this advantage, they do not know what they need to learn. So where do our mystics end up? The hospital psychiatric wards are the only haven for these individuals. The blind leading the blind.

The initiate must seek out his or her own teachers, a task that takes persistence and skill. I have told you of Natalie Rogers, a therapist with an unusually different technique from other therapists I have gone to. She uses her intuitive knowledge of her own being in order to reflect the true image of the person she deals with. In other words, she is able to "see" without her eyes, "hear" without her ears. These are the characteristics of a true mystic; and indeed, Natalie Rogers is of this class.

THE SCIENCE OF MIND AND BODY

During my manic episodes, it was an immense effort for me to try to control my mind as it was running away. To see what it was like for me, clench your hand tightly into a fist. How long can you sustain it? A few seconds, perhaps; certainly not more than a few minutes. Now imagine maintaining that same degree of control over your mind for days, without once letting up the tension. The entire being is stressed.

At different times during therapy I experienced major releases of stress. These releases unlocked an immense amount of energy that had to be channeled into acceptable outlets. When this first occurred, I found it almost impossible to sleep. Then I began to worry that I was not sleeping. My solution, which I thought was a logical one, was to release this energy through exercise until it was spent. I expected to be exhausted and able to sleep. But this solution turned out to be no solution at all. Instead of dispersing the energy, it produced a vacuum that drew into itself more energy, thus causing a dangerous, endless cycle. Somewhat by chance I discovered that the solution was the exact opposite. It involved sitting down and meditating, letting this energy settle down sufficiently that it could be redirected for other uses.

When I first tried meditating, it was almost impossible for me to do. My body wanted to move, my mind wanted to think. Meditation took a conscious effort. But the results were astounding. Once the energy was allowed to settle down, I was able, over a period of several days, to channel it into constructive expression in other areas of my life. The newly released energy seemed to have a vitality of its own.

This book is just one of the projects that came out of the proper release and channeling of this energy.

Meditation is comparable to the contraction of the fist in the exercise I described. But instead of being an active force that relies on tension to maintain control—a control that cannot be sustained for any length of time—it is a passive force that can be maintained through the use of the will almost indefinitely. This is a major point for consideration. It is the only way for the newly released energy to be powered down to a level where it can be used constructively. Meditation acts as the transformer in this exchange of heat for light.

Since the body and the mind are interconnected, I would like to say something about body work. Every thought and feeling that we experience also has a physical effect on the body. Humans capture and hold on to emotional disturbances in the muscles of the body, producing physical stress. Over the past two decades, we have been swamped with methods for body work—Rolfing, Shiatsu, the Trager method, and so on. All these systems are designed to release stress that has accumulated in the body. Many of us have accumulated so much stress that we need a trained body worker to assist us in removing these blocks.

We as a society have never been taught how to avoid this accumulation of stress. When it builds to the point that it is noticed, we are told to take a vacation. But there has always existed a way to avoid the build-up of mental and physical stress. That is the way of Raja yoga, the science of physical and mental control. Asanas, which are the physical postures that an individual assumes during yoga, allow the individual to perform self-body work without a trainer. The individual who practices the asanas is manipulating the body, which through its own physical condition will control the flow of release. The various physical postures, when held correctly, produce the right amount of pressure to break through blockages in the body, thus releasing trapped energy. Once the energy is released, meditation is used to transform this energy so that it can be used in a constructive way.

I strongly believe that the yoga practices that exist today can and should be used by anyone traveling the conscious path toward the union of the self with the Self. You do not have to lock yourself away in an ashram and live the life of a pure yogi. If we learn the tools that the yogis use, we can then incorporate these tools into our own lives.

This is my story. My journey started in the dark and was without direction until I asked the question, What if? What if mania is not an illness but an initiation into our psychic birthright? What if we are not only humans having a spiritual experience, but also spiritual beings having a human experience? My journey has taken me from the darkness of ignorance to the light of understanding, an understanding of who and what I am. It is a never-ending story that we all live.

I would like to close with some thoughts from Robert Bly. In *Iron John,* Bly said,

[W]here a man's wound is, that is where his genius will be . . . that is precisely the place from which we give our major gift to the community.

I have entered my wound, and this is my gift.

PEACE AND GREAT SPIRITS

Bibliography

Assagioli, Roberto. *Act of Will.* New York: Penguin Books USA Inc., 1973.

Assagioli, Roberto. *Psychosynthesis.* SterlingLord Literistic, Inc., New York: Viking Penguin, 1965.

Bly, Robert. *Iron John.* Reading, MA: Addison-Wesley Publishing Company, 1990.

Bryson, John (ed.). *Matthew Arnold Poetry and Prose.* Cambridge, MA: Harvard University Press, 1963.

Bucke, Richard. *Cosmic Consciousness.* New York: E.P.Dutton Publishing Company, 1923.

Campbell, Joseph and Moyers, Bill. *The Power of Myth.* New York: Doubleday, 1988.

Colbin, Annemarie. *Food and Healing.* New York: Ballantine, 1986.

Dumont, Theron. *The Master Mind.* Homewood, IL: Yoga Publication Society, 1918.

Dumont, Theron. *The Power of Concentration.* Homewood, IL: Yoga Publication Society, 1918.

Fieve, Ronald. *Moodswing.* New York: William Morrow & Company, Inc., 1975.

Hamilton, Edith. *Mythology.* Boston: Little Brown, 1942.

Hudson, Thompson J. *The Law of Psychic Phenomena.* Salinas, CA: Hudson-Cohan Publishing Company, 1893.

Huxley, Aldous. *The Doors of Perception.* New York: Harper & Row Publishers, 1954.

Jamison, Kay Redfield. *Touched with Fire.* New York: The Free Press, 1993.

Jung, Carl. *The Archetypes and the Collective Unconscious.* Princeton, NJ: Princeton University Press, 1969.

Jung, Carl. *Introduction to a Science of Mythology.* New York: Chapman and Hall Inc., 1951.

Kast, Verena. *Imagination as Space of Freedom.* New York: Fromm International Publising Corp., 1993.

Keen, Sam. *Fire in the Belly.* New York: Bantam Books, 1991.

Keirsey, David and Bates, Marilyn. *Please Understand Me.* Del Mar, CA: Prometheus Nemesis Book Company, 1978.

Mandell, Marshall and Scanlon, Lynne. *5-Day Allergy Relief System.* New York: Simon & Schuster, 1979.

Maslow, Abraham. *Further Reaches of the Human Nature.* New York: Penguin Books, Inc., 1971.

Meditations on the Tarot. Rockport, MA: Element Books, 1985.

Moore, Thomas. *Care of the Soul.* New York: HarperCollins Publishers, Inc., 1992.

Moore, Robert and Gillette, Douglas. *King, Warrior, Magician, Lover.* New York: HarperCollins Publishers, Inc., 1990.

Moore, Robert and Gillette, Douglas. *The King Within.* New York: William Morrow and Company, 1992.

Muktananda, Swami. *Play of Consciousness.* SYDA Foundation, 1978.

Ouspensky, P.D. *Tertium Organum.* New York: Random House, Inc., 1920.

Peale, Norman. *Enthusiasm Makes the Difference.* New York: Simon & Schuster, Inc., 1967.

Peris, Frederick. *Gestalt Therapy Verbatim.* Moab, UT: Real People Press, 1959.

Stallone, James and Migdal, Sy. *Growing Sane.* Dallas, PA: Upshur Press, 1991.

Steiner, Rudolf. *Knowledge of the Higher Worlds and its Attainment.* Hudson, NY: Anthroposophic Press, Inc., 1947.

Tannen, Deborah. *You Just Don't Understand.* New York: Ballantine Books, 1990.

Underhill, Evelyn. *Mysticism, Methien and Company.* LTD, 1911.

Yates, Frances. *Giordano Bruno and the Hermetic Tradition.* Chicago: University of Chicago Press, 1964.

Yates, Frances. *DSM-III-R.* Washington, D.C., American Psychiatric Association, 1987.

Index